BELONG
—— *with* ——
KONGLISH

A GUIDE TO UNDERSTANDING KOREAN-STYLE ENGLISH AND AVOIDING COMMON MISCOMMUNICATIONS

LAUREN GREEN
WITH YIRE LEE

Library of Congress Number: 2024910106

First paperback edition November 2024

ISBN 979-8-9899078-3-0 (Paperback)
ISBN 979-8-9899078-5-4 (Hardcover)
ISBN 979-8-9899078-4-7 (eBook)

Lauren's Language Lessons, LLC
Houston, Texas, USA
www.LaurensLanguageLessons.com

TABLE OF CONTENTS

INTRODUCTION 7

1 ABBREVIATIONS 11

    A/S AFTER SERVICE 12

    APPL(E) 13

    BGM 13

    BJ 14

    CF 15

    D/C 15

    EMS 16

    KK 16

    OST 17

    SF 17

    PT 18

    PPT 19

    TT OR TT TT 20

    ^^ 21

2 FOOD & DRINKS 23

    AMERICANO 24

    BAR 25

    BBQ 25

    CAN MAEKJU 26

    CHICKEN 26

    CIDER 27

    CHOCO(L) 28

    COLA / KOLA 28

    COMBI 29

    COMBO SET 29

    CREAM PASTA 30

    HOP/HOF 30

    HOT DOG 31

    JELLY 32

    ICE BAR 33

    LIVE BEER 33

    LUNCHBOX 34

    MENU 34

    ONE SHOT 35

    PUDDING 35

    SAND 36

    SAUCE CHICKEN 37

    SAUCE 38

    YOGURT 38

YOPLAIT 39

ZERO COLA 39

3 CLOTHING & FASHION 41

    BIG SIZE 42

    BURBERRY / BURBERRY CHECK MUNI 42

    COMBI-STYLE 43

    COUPLE LOOK 43

    FREE SIZE 44

    DRESS 45

    GOLDEN PANTS / CORDON PANTS 45

    GOWN 46

    HALF COAT 47

    JACKU 47

    JUMPER 48

    SCHOOL JUMPER 48

    MUFFLER 49

    ONE PIECE 50

    PANTY 51

    PANTY STOCKINGS 52

    PADDING 52

    POLAR T 53

    S SIZE 53

    M SIZE 54

    L SIZE 54

    LL SIZE OR 2L 55

    LLL SIZE OR 3L 55

    SEPARATE CODI 56

    SINGLE STYLE SUIT 56

    SLIPPERS 57

    TRAINING (BOK) 58

    TWO PIECE 59

    WALKER 60

    Y SHIRT 60

4 ACCESSORIES 61

    CROSS BAG 62

    HAIR BAND 62

    HAIR PIN 63

    MANICURE 64

    RIBBON 65

    SACK 65

5 MAKEUP & SKINCARE 67

CUSHION 68
EYE REMOVER 68
PACK 69
RINSE 70
ROUGE 70
SKIN 71

6 BODY & PHYSICAL APPEARANCE 73

BODYLINE 74
DOUBLE EYELID 75
GLAMOUR 76
HIP 76
LOSE MY/YOUR WEIGHT 77
IMAGE 78
OUTLOOK 78
S-LINE 79
V-LINE 79
VISUAL 80

7 HEALTH 81

BALANCED MEAL 82
BAND 82
CONDITION 83
CHECK UP 84
DIET 84
DISK 85
FITNESS 86
GARGLE 86
GYPS 87
HEALING TIME 87
HEALTH 88
HEALTHY MEAL 88
HOSPITAL 89
MR 90
OVEREAT 90
PASS 91
PAY DOCTOR 91
RINGER 92
SUNCREAM 92
WELL BEING 93

8 SCHOOL, WORK, & THE OFFICE 95

ACADEMIC CLASS 96
ACADEMY 97
BALL PEN 97

BLUE WORKER 98
BOND 98
CIRCLE 99
CLIP 99
COURSE 100
CUNNING 100
DIARY 101
ENGINEER 101
HARD BOARD 102
HOTCHKISS 102
JUNIOR 103
LETTERING 104
MAGIC 104
NAME PEN 105
NAME CARD 105
NOTE 106
NOTEBOOK 106
OFFICER 107
ONE BY ONE 108
PRINT 108
READ LOUD 109
SALARYMAN 109
SENIOR 110
SHARP 112
SIGN PEN 112
SPECS 113
TRAINING 113
WHITE 114
WHITE WORKER 114
WORKING LEVEL PEOPLE 115

9 TECHNOLOGY 117

COMPUTER 118
DIKA 118
FLASH 119
GAME ROOM /PC BAR / PC ROOM 119
GMAP 120
HAND PHONE 120
HOMEPI 121
ID OR MEMBER ID 121
NAVI/NAVIGATION 122
PC 122
SECRET NUMBER 123
SELCA 123
SELF-CAM 124

10 **MONEY** **125**

    BIG MONEY 126

    FUND 126

    POCKET MONEY 127

    POOR 127

    RENTAL FEE 128

    SMALL MONEY 128

11 **SHOPPING**.................................**129**

    BARGAIN 130

    CORNER 130

    DEPART / DEPARTMENT 131

    DOZ 131

    EYE SHOPPING 132

    GROCERY 132

    HANDMADE 133

    MAKER 133

    MART 134

    ONE PLUS ONE 134

    PART 135

    SELF 136

    SERVICE 136

    SUPER 137

12 **HOUSE, HOMES, & LIVING**.................**139**

    AIR CON 140

    APART (APT) 140

    CARPET 141

    CLOSET 141

    CONSENT 142

    DRESS ROOM 142

    INTERPHONE 143

    MY ROOM 143

    ONE ROOM 144

    OFFICETEL 144

    OUTSIDE 145

    ROX/LOX 146

    SENIOR TOWN 148

    SILVER TOWN 148

    SHOWER BATH 149

    SHOWER BOOTH 149

    STAND 150

    VERANDA 150

13 **APPLIANCES**................................ **151**

    COOKER 152

DRYER 152

GAS RANGE 153

INDUCTION 153

MIXER 154

REFRIDGE 154

STAINLESS 155

REMO CON / REMOTE CON 155

14 **SOCIAL LIFE**.................................**157**

    EVENT 158

    FAMILY NAME 159

    NIGHT 159

    SCHEDULE 160

    SILLY 161

    SNS 162

    UNTACT 162

15 **RELATIONSHIPS & DATING**.............**163**

    BOOKING 164

    HUNTING 164

    MEETING 165

    MY/OUR COUPLE (OUR BOO BOO) 165

    PROPOSE 166

    SKINSHIP 166

    SOLO 167

    THEIR EYES ARE HIGH 167

    WEDDING MARCH 168

16 **FEELINGS, EMOTIONS, DESCRIBING CHARACTER & PERSONALITY**.............**169**

    CENTI 170

    CHEER UP 170

    CHIC 171

    COMPLEX 171

    FIGHTING 172

    FROZEN 172

    MANIA 173

    MENTAL 173

    MIND 174

    MIND CONTROL 174

    MULTI-PLAYER 175

17 **SPORTS & ACTIVITIES**.........................**177**

    BACK NUMBER 178

    BICYCLE HIKING..............................179

    HANDY 179

Hiking 180
Pocketball 181
Running Machine 181
Skin Scuba 182
Sports Dancing 182
Sportsman 183
Trekking 183

18 **MUSIC, MOVIES, TV, &**
ENTERTAINMENT 185

Back Dancer 186
Back Singer 186
Chorus 187
CM Song 187
Docu 188
Drama 188
Episode 189
Fan Sign or Fan Signing 189
Fantastic 190
Gagman/Gagwoman 190
Highteen Star 191
Melodrama 191
Pierrot 192
Sign 193
Talent 193
Telebi 194
Top Star 194
TV Show 195

19 **TRAVEL** 197

Carrier 198
Goods 198
Hand(y) Carry 199
Hocance 199
Morning Call 200
Outing 200
Rounding 201
Top, Tap 202

20 **CARS & TRANSPORTATION**............203

Accel 204
Autobi 204
Back Mirror 205
Caravan 205

Camping Car 206
Car Center 207
Claxon 207
Handle 208
Kickboard 208
Mission 209
Open Car 209
Punk 210
Radiator 210
Scooter 211
Side Brake 211
Sticker 212
Window Brush / Wiper..................... 212

21 **TOOLS & OTHER USEFUL ITEMS**....213

Driver 214
MacGyver Knife 215
Pincher 215
Poklain 216
Tuppa 216
Vinyl 217
Wrap 217
Zipper Bag 218

22 **MISCELLANEOUS**....................................219

Dry 220
Journal 220
One Shot, One Kill 221
Over 221
Pick Me Up 222
Paradigm 223
Revive 223
Shadow 224
Speak Out 224
Unisex 225

Acknowledgments 227
Image Credits 229
Bibliography 230
Index...231
About the Author.............................. 233
About Lauren's Language Lessons . 233
About the Translator......................... 234

INTRODUCTION: WHY I WROTE THIS BOOK

I once had a student from Korea who told me her son was an officer. For months, I thought her son was a police officer in Korea. At one point, we were talking about him, and I asked, "Is it dangerous to be an officer in Korea?" She looked really confused. "Of course not." I later found out he worked for a government agency in the finance department and that "officer" did not mean the same thing to Koreans as it did to me. Something had been lost in translation.

During my early years of teaching English to Koreans, I noticed that students would often say English words that didn't fit into the context of our conversation and didn't make sense. "He did overeat yesterday, so he can't come to class today." I'd feel confused and try to ask clarifying questions to understand their meanings. "I don't understand why the amount he ate yesterday is related to whether he is coming to class today..." Students would feel frustrated, wondering why I didn't understand the English they were speaking. One student even said quite bluntly in exasperation, "I am speaking English, why don't you understand me? Is it my accent?" In reality, he was speaking Konglish.

Konglish, or Korean-style English, is a fascinating version of English spoken in South Korea, much like Singlish in Singapore, Kongish in Hong Kong, or Japanglish in Japan. It includes Koreanized English words with similar meanings to their original English counterparts and just slightly different pronunciations (*pizza*). However, Konglish also includes hundreds of English words that have completely different meanings in Korean English than they do in American English (*consent*). Sometimes, there are even words that are neither Korean nor English (*Pierrot*). Additionally, many terms are technically English but in practicality don't exist at all (*salaryman*) while others are creative abbreviations that are not used or understood outside of Korea (*CF*).

In many ways, Konglish often provides a sense of identity for the Korean community within the United States and other countries, building unity and connection. In South Korea, Konglish reflects a piece of Korea's unique culture and serves as an intriguing and evolving example of the ever-changing world of language and our ever-growing global connectedness. However, outside of Korean communities themselves, the Korean version of English gets lost in translation, and misunderstandings abound.

Virtually every American who has spent significant time in South Korea can tell you a story about a language misunderstanding while speaking English with someone who was otherwise fluent. In Korea, a business partner will be quick to offer you his or her **name card** before inviting you to the **hop** to drink soju **one shot**. A friend may be envious of someone's **S-line** or **V-line**. Someone might tell you they love to eat **sand** at the beach, and you will likely come across doctors who prefer to give shots in a patient's **hip**.

The purpose of this book is to serve as a guide for English speakers who spend time speaking English with South Koreans. The aim is to help avoid some of the miscommunications that are often encountered when one is unfamiliar with Konglish. Maybe you are a businessperson regularly working alongside Korean companies; maybe you plan to teach in South Korea; maybe you work closely with a Korean expat or immigrant community; maybe you love Korean culture like K-pop and K-dramas; maybe you're planning a trip to Korea, or maybe you just love learning about other cultures and languages... Then this book is for you.

You will learn many words that have different meanings in Korean English (Konglish) and in American English and others that are technically English but only exist in South Korea. You will likely find that a few words in this book simply come from British-style English (*diary, caravan*) and have similar meanings when spoken in the UK and in South Korea but different meanings when spoken in North America. You will also hear some personal stories of my own confusion with Konglish along with a few cultural pointers that I've learned along the way. My hope is that this book will help you understand your friends, clients, coworkers, and favorite celebrities more clearly and avoid some of these potential miscommunications!

If you are a native Korean speaker wishing to speak English more clearly to your American or Canadian friends, please check out *Wronglish Konglish: A Guide to Avoiding Miscommunications when Speaking English to North Americans*.

Special Note 1: *Language is constantly changing! Even in the years of writing and putting together this book, new Konglish words have been adopted; older Konglish words have* become outdated, and some previously obscure Konglish words have become mainstream and commonly used even in American English circles.

It's also important to keep in mind that English itself is extremely diverse. This book focuses on the differences between American English and Korean English and does not address the differences that may be found between Konglish and other varieties of English. However, even within the United States, there can be regional differences in certain word choices as well as differences based on age, generation, socioeconomics, life experiences, subculture, ethnic background, field of work, and much more. You may find that depending on your own language background, your usage of the included terms may differ slightly.

This book is not meant to serve as a complete dictionary, rather a helpful resource, and I have included the most common, useful, or relevant information. With those caveats listed above, I have done my best to make this book as extensive as possible, knowing that because of the diversity of English itself and the ever-changing nature of language, it will never be completely possible for this book to be truly all-inclusive.

Special Note 2: It's helpful to keep in mind that some Korean consonants do not correspond exactly with one English letter. As a result, there can sometimes be slight differences in romanization of terms. As an example, the pronunciation of the Korean "ㄹ" is somewhere in between that of an "L" and "R", and the pronunciation of the Korean "ㄱ" is somewhere between that of an English "G" and "K". As an example, the term 골덴바지 may be translated to English as "Golden Pants" or "Cordon Pants" where the actual Korean pronunciation would be somewhere in between those two words.

Special Note 3: You will find that the terms "Korean" and "South Korean" as well as "Korea" and "South Korea" are used interchangeably in this book. Many people from South Korea simply use the terms "Korea" and "Korean," often leaving Westerners confused with the question, "North Korea or South Korea?" In this book, you may assume that any usage of the word "Korea" refers to South Korea, and any usage of the word "Korean" refers to South Korean.

Special Thanks to Yire Lee for her extensive help in the development of this book and her diligent work in translating its counterpart for Korean speakers (*Wronglish Konglish: A Guide to Avoiding Miscommunications when Speaking English with North Americans*).

NOTE ABOUT QR CODES: Scan the QR code located on each chapter title page to hear audio for Korean pronunciation of the words included in each chapter! For a continuous playlist of all chapters and words included in this book, scan this QR code →

1

ABBREVIATIONS

Scan for Audio

A/S After Service
에이 에스 / 에프터 서비스

Meaning in Konglish:

A warranty on a product or free help or service after purchasing a product

Example Konglish Sentence:

I just bought this phone one week ago, but it is not working correctly. Do you have _A/S_?

Translated to American English:

I just bought this phone one week ago, but it is not working correctly. Does it have a _warranty_? / Is it under _warranty_?

A/S in the U.S.

I once had a student who moved to the United States and bought a couch. A week later she found a small rip in one of the cushions. She went to the store and asked if they had A/S on her sofa purchase. The store employees looked at her kind of strangely and eventually went to get a manager to help. "A/S. After service," she asked again, "Do you have after service for my couch?" Still, no one at the store understood. She left the store feeling sad and defeated and thought maybe her accent was too thick for people to understand. She was sure she was speaking correct English.

APPL(E) 어플

Meaning in Konglish:
App

Example Konglish Sentence:
Kakao *appl(e)* is the most widely used *appl(e)* in Korea.

Translated to American English:
The Kakao *app* is the most widely used *app* in Korea.

BGM 비지엠

Meaning in Konglish:
An abbreviation for background music

Example Konglish Sentence:
That *CF* is famous for its *BGM*.

Translated to American English:
That *commercial* is famous for its *background music*.

BJ 비제이

Meaning in Konglish:

Abbreviation for broadcasting jockey. This is someone like a YouTuber or live streamer who provides live content like games, music, commentaries, narration, etc., often over a live streamed event or show.

Example Konglish Sentence:

My friend is a _BJ_ on YouTube.

Translated to American English:

My friend is a _YouTube streamer_. My friend is a _live streamer_.

Origins

BJ is an abbreviation of the English words _broadcast_ and _jockey_. The author guesses this may come from a mixing of terms _broadcast announcer_ or _radio broadcasting_ and _disc jockey (DJ)_.

CF 씨에프

Meaning in Konglish:

Commercial or Ad on TV

Example Konglish Sentence:

That _CF_ is famous for its _BGM_.

Translated to American English:

That _commercial_ is famous for its _background music_.

D/C 디씨

Meaning in South Korea:

Discount

Example Konglish Sentence:

If you purchase more than five items,
I can give you _D/C_.

Translated to American English:

If you purchase more than five items, I can give you a _discount_.

EMS 이엠에스

Meaning in Konglish:

Ambulance

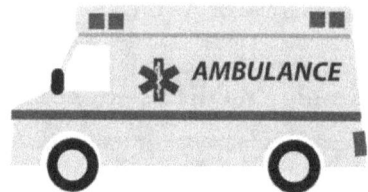

Example Konglish Sentence:

I hear an _EMS_ nearby.

Translated to American English:

I hear an _ambulance_ nearby.

Kk ㅋㅋ

Meaning in Konglish:

Lol or Haha or Hahahaha

Example Konglish Sentence:

Kkkkkk

Translated to American English:

Hahahahahahaha

Laughing in Korean

The number of k's relates to how funny something is, like using haha for something mildly funny or hahahaha for something very funny.

OST 오에스티

Meaning in Konglish:

Movie soundtrack (OST stands for Original Soundtrack)

Example Konglish Sentence:

Korean dramas use famous singers for their _OSTs_.

Translated to American English:

Korean dramas use famous singers for their _soundtracks_.

SF 에스에프

Meaning in Konglish:

Science fiction

Example Konglish Sentence:

I love a _SF_ novel.

Translated to American English:

I love _science fiction_ books.

I love _sci-fi_ novels.

PT 피티

Meaning in Konglish:

1. Presentation (e.g., a PowerPoint presentation)
2. Personal trainer

Example Konglish Sentence:

I have a class with my _PT_ teacher today. / I have a _PT_ class today.

Mr. Lee will give a _PT_ at tomorrow's meeting.

Translated to American English:

I have a session with my _personal trainer_ today.

Mr. Lee will give a _presentation_ at tomorrow's meeting.

The First PT

One day, I was teaching a business English class for several Korean businessmen. As they were arriving for my class, one student said, "Mr. Kim has a PT first today." Thinking he meant that Mr. Kim had been hurt and perhaps had a physical therapy session that overlapped with our class, I asked, "Oh really? So will he miss our class today or just be a little late? Is he OK?" The student looked confused. "No, he is here. He will do a PT first... the homework you gave us." I scratched my head. The only homework I had given them was to do a business-related PowerPoint presentation. Turns out, that's what he meant! And before we started our presentations, I taught them that _PT_ does not mean "presentation" in American English. They were all shocked to learn this new information, and I was equally shocked to learn that in Korea, _PT_ can mean "presentation."

PPT 피피티

Meaning in Konglish:

PowerPoint presentation or slideshow

Example Konglish Sentence:

He is going to prepare a *PPT* for the meeting.

Translated to American English:

He is going to prepare a *PowerPoint presentation* for the meeting.

Family Reunion PPT

Recently, one of my Korean American friends who was born and raised in the United States went back to Korea with her husband and children for the first time in many years for a wedding and family reunion. Though she speaks Korean, her husband and children don't speak Korean at all, so most of her cousins speak to them in English. When my friend's family arrived in Seoul for the family reunion and were greeted by relatives, one of her cousins proudly explained that he had prepared a wonderful PPT for their family reunion. None of them knew what this meant, but they were excited to find out. It turns out, the cousins had put together a heart-warming PowerPoint slideshow of family pictures throughout the years, including photos of cousins, aunts, and uncles back into their childhoods.

TT OR TT TT ㅠ ㅠ

Meaning in Konglish:

Really sad face :(

Example Konglish Sentence:

Teacher, I'm sorry, I can't come to class today. I have an appointment at the dentist. I'm sorry ㅠ ㅠ

Are you going to Jessica's birthday party tomorrow? I really wanted to go, but I have to work all day ㅠ I heard it's going to be so fun ㅠ ㅠ

Translated to American English:

Teacher, I'm sorry, I can't come to class today. I have an appointment at the dentist. I'm sorry :(

Are you going to Jessica's birthday party tomorrow? I really wanted to go, but I have to work all day :(I heard it's going to be so fun :(:(

Korean Life & Culture: "Teacher"

In Korea, it is considered respectful to only address a teacher as "*Seonsaengnim*" or "Teacher." In the United States, I've met many teachers who find it extremely rude when students address them this way. I know a few who will follow this with a snarky response such as, "Excuse you, did you forget my name?" If you teach or plan to teach English in Korea, it will be important to remember that students by default will avoid addressing you by name in order to show respect. Similarly, if you are a teacher in the United States working with students from Korea, please understand that a student addressing you as only "Teacher" is not trying to disrespect you and may be unaware of the custom of addressing teachers as Mr. Lastname.

Meaning in Konglish:

:)

Example Konglish Sentence:

Hello ^^.

Translated to American English:

Hello :)

A Friendly Boss

I once had a Korean boss. She emailed me some important information and wrote ^^ in a sentence at the end of the email. I reread the whole email multiple times trying to figure out what details I may have missed previously that she wanted me to revisit. I couldn't find anything I might have been missing. I eventually asked a Korean friend what ^^ meant, and she told me it was basically a smiley face. I laughed in relief as I explained how stressed out I had been trying to figure out what information "above" in the email my boss wanted me to find. I had no idea she was just being friendly and typing a smiley face emoji.

FOOD AND DRINKS

AMERICANO 아메리카노

Meaning in Konglish:

Americano or simply American-style coffee, including drip coffee brewed in a coffee machine or black coffee

Note: A-a 아아 *(ah-ah) is a newer abbreviation meaning iced Americano*

Example Konglish Sentence:

Americans drink *Americanos*, not espresso like many Koreans.

Translated to American English:

Americans drink *drip coffee*, not espresso like many Koreans.

"Americans Love Americanos!"

If you are an American in Korea and mention you are a coffee-drinker, be prepared for many people to assume you love Americanos. In my early days of teaching, I often had Korean students surprise me with coffee, especially during our early morning classes. I love coffee, but Americano is never my personal preference. However, 9 times out of 10, when my students surprised me with coffee, they proudly declared, "We brought you American coffee! We know Americans love Americanos!" Don't get me wrong, I was very thankful for the coffee and the kind students who went out of their way to give me my caffeine fix for the day; I just didn't know how to tell them without sounding ungrateful that not all Americans love Americanos. Eventually I got creative and taught a lesson on hospitality and etiquette in American culture which included asking, "How do you like your coffee?" and "What kind of coffee do you like?"

BAR 바 (술집)

Meaning in Konglish:

Usually a drinks-only bar for those of legal drinking age; a lounge, a club

Example Konglish Sentence:

I was shocked when an American friend told me you can take your kids to the _bar_, but when we arrived I realized it was just a _hop_.

Translated to American English:

I was shocked when an American friend told me you can take your kids to the _lounge/club_, but when we arrived, I realized it was just a _bar and grill for all ages_.

BBQ 비비큐

Meaning in Konglish:

Barbecued meats but not Korean-style BBQ. In Konglish, BBQ is pronounced like the letters B-B-Q rather than the word "barbecue."

Example Konglish Sentence:

We ate _B-B-Q_.

Translated to American English:

We ate _barbecue_.

CAN MAEKJU 캔 맥주

Meaning in Konglish:

Canned beer

Example Konglish Sentence:

Do you prefer _can maekju_, bottled beer, or live beer?

Translated to American English:

Do you prefer _canned beer_, bottled beer, or beer on tap?

CHICKEN 치킨

Meaning in Konglish:

Fried chicken

Example Konglish Sentence:

We always eat _chicken_ on Fridays.

Translated to American English:

We always eat _fried chicken_ on Fridays.

CIDER 사이다

Meaning in Konglish:

A non-alcoholic fizzy citrus soft drink similar to and including Sprite and 7UP

Example Konglish Sentence:

Cider is great because it doesn't have alcohol and can help your stomach feel better. It's also great for kids. Americans drink _cider_ when they are sick.

Translated to American English:

Sprite is great because it doesn't have alcohol and can help your stomach feel better. It's also great for kids. Americans drink _Sprite_ or _7UP_ when they are sick.

The Advantage

I had a student who was a businessman and often golfed with colleagues on the weekend when he lived in the United States. He and his colleagues had an ongoing friendly competition. One particular day, he was determined to win, so he devised a simple plan. While his colleagues ordered beer, he would order cider. "All my colleagues will be affected by the alcohol, but I will have an advantage since cider isn't alcoholic," he schemed proudly to himself. Believing he was ordering something akin to Sprite, he was surprised when he received a dark bottle with an apple on it and thought, "Wow, I guess cider in the U.S. is made with apples and served in a glass bottle! It must be much nicer here!" After several bottles, he noticed that his score wasn't much better than usual, and he was feeling a little tipsy. "It must be the heat outside today," he guessed. He had no idea that cider in the United States wasn't a Sprite-like drink and can have around 4-5% alcohol, similar to beer. Needless to say, he didn't have much of an advantage in golfing that day.

CHOCO(L) 초코 (초콜)

Meaning in Konglish:

Short for chocolate

Example Konglish Sentence:

Do you want some *choco*?

Translated to American English:

Do you want some *chocolate*?

COLA / KOLA 콜라

Meaning in Konglish:

Coke

Example Konglish Sentence:

I'd like a *cola* to drink.

Translated to American English:

I'd like a *Coke* to drink.

COMBI 콤비

Meaning in Konglish:

1. Supreme pizza
2. A pizza with different toppings on each half/quarter

Example Konglish Sentence:

My favorite pizza is _combi pizza_.

Translated to American English:

My favorite pizza is _supreme pizza_.

COMBO SET 콤보세트

Meaning in Konglish:

Combo or Meal

Example Konglish Sentence:

Thanks for your hamburger order at LBurger.

Would you like to make that a _combo set_ or just the burger?

Translated to American English:

Thanks for your hamburger order at LBurger.

Would you like to make that a _combo_/_meal_ or just the burger?

CREAM PASTA 크림 파스타

Meaning in Konglish:

Alfredo pasta or any pasta dish with a cream sauce

Example Konglish Sentence:

That restaurant has good _cream pasta_.

Translated to American English:

That restaurant has good _Alfredo pasta_.

HOP/HOF 호프

Meaning in Konglish:

A bar or pub

Example Konglish Sentence:

We like going to that _hop_ after work. They have good beer and pizza.

Translated to American English:

We like going to that _bar_ after work. They have good beer and pizza.

HOT DOG 핫도그

Meaning in Konglish:

A sausage on a stick that's lightly breaded and fried. It's similar to an American corn dog, but it is often covered with lots of interesting and creative toppings and textures to create different delicious flavor profiles!

Example Konglish Sentence:

I love _hot dogs_ because they are on a stick and are easy to eat.

Translated to American English:

I love _corn dogs_ because they are on a stick and are easy to eat.

JELLY 젤리

Meaning in Konglish:

Gummies, gummy bears, jello

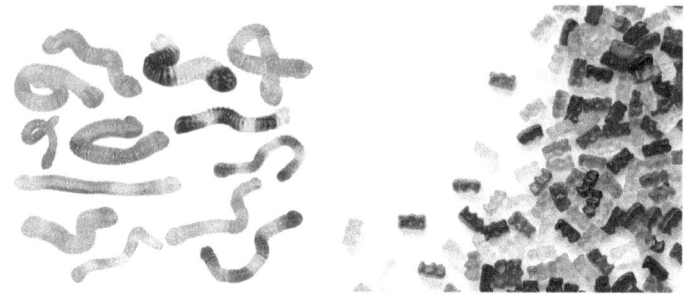

Example Konglish Sentence:

Kids love _jelly_.

I love taking _jelly_ vitamins.

Translated to American English:

Kids love _gummies_. / Kids love _jello_.

I love taking _gummy_ vitamins.

ICE BAR 아이스 바

Meaning in Konglish:

Popsicle, ice cream bar, frozen juice bar

Example Konglish Sentence:

Ice bars are an exciting treat for kids in Korea in
the summer.

Translated to American English:

Popsicles are an exciting treat for kids in Korea in
the summer.

LIVE BEER 생맥주

Meaning in Konglish:

Beer on tap rather than from a can or bottle

Example Konglish Sentence:

That bar has good _live beer_.
I'd like to order _live beer_.
What _live beers_ do you have?

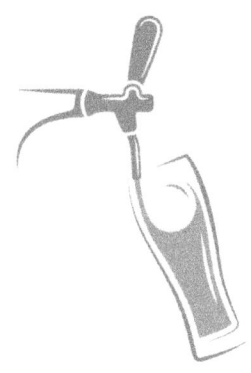

Translated to American English:

That bar has good _draft beer_.
I'd like to order the _draft beer_.
What beers do you have _on tap_?

LUNCHBOX 런치박스

Meaning in Konglish:

A homemade lunch brought to work or school. Lunchbox refers more to the food rather than the box itself.

Example Konglish Sentence:

He brought his _lunchbox_ to work.

We ate a _lunchbox_ for lunch.

Translated to American English:

He brought his _lunch_ to work.

We ate a _homemade lunch_ / _lunch from home_.

MENU 메뉴

Meaning in Konglish:

This can mean menu, the whole list of food, but it can also mean each separate item at a restaurant that is offered. It's common for Koreans to ask, "What menu did you order at the restaurant?" meaning "What did you order to eat?"

Example Konglish Sentence:

What _menu_ did you order?

Translated to American English:

What did you order?

ONE SHOT 원샷

Meaning in Konglish:

In Korea, you say this phrase when you are drinking (especially soju) and taking a shot very quickly. It can sometimes be similar to "Cheers!"

Example Konglish Sentence:

You have to drink soju *one shot*.

Here, have some soju! *One shot*!

Translated to American English:

You have to drink soju *like (you're doing) a shot*.

Here, have some soju! *Cheers*!

PUDDING 푸딩

Meaning in Konglish:

Jello and pudding

Example Konglish Sentence:

I like the fruit inside the *pudding*.

Translated to American English:

I like the fruit inside the *jello*.

SAND 샌드

Meaning in Konglish:

A stuffed cookie or sandwich cookie like an Oreo, ice cream cookie, or ice cream sandwich (e.g., cookie sand, chocolate sand cookie) or a shortened name of any specialty sandwich (e.g., egg sand, tofu sand)

Example Konglish Sentence:

At the beach, they sell good _sand_.

Translated to American English:

At the beach, they sell good _ice cream sandwiches_.

At the beach, they sell good _sandwich cookies_.

SAUCE CHICKEN 양념치킨

Meaning in Konglish:

Korean-style fried chicken with sauce. This is similar to what Americans call wings, but they can be made from other parts of the chicken too, not just the wings. They're also slightly more crispy than typical American wings.

Example Konglish Sentence:

We love eating _sauce chicken_ after work.

Translated to American English:

We love eating _Korean-style fried chicken with sauce_ after work.

We love eating _Korean-style wings_ after work.

We love eating _Korean chicken_ after work.

SAUCE 소스

Meaning in Konglish:

Salad dressing or sauce or condiments like ketchup and mustard

Example Konglish Sentence:

Do you put _sauce_ on your salad?
I always use _sauce_.

Translated to American English:

Do you put _salad dressing_ on your salad?
I always use _salad dressing_.

YOGURT 요구르트

Meaning in Konglish:

Liquid probiotic yogurt drink

Example Konglish Sentence:

I noticed that many stores in the USA only sell Yoplait but not _yogurt_.

Translated to American English:

I noticed that many stores in the USA only sell yogurt and not _liquid probiotic yogurt_.

YOPLAIT 요플레

Meaning in Konglish:

Yogurt, any brand

Example Konglish Sentence:

I noticed that many stores in the USA only sell _Yoplait_ but not yogurt.

Translated to American English:

I noticed that many stores in the USA only sell _yogurt_ but not liquid probiotic yogurt.

ZERO COLA 제로 콜라

Meaning in Konglish:

Diet Coke or Coke Zero

Example Konglish Sentence:

Do you have a _zero cola_?

Translated to American English:

Do you have a _Diet Coke_?

CLOTHING AND FASHION

3

Scan for Audio

BIG SIZE 빅사이즈

Meaning in Konglish:

Plus size clothing

Example Konglish Sentence:

Do you sell _big size_ here?

Translated to American English:

Do you sell _plus size_ clothes here?

BURBERRY / BURBERRY CHECK MUNI
버버리/버버리 체크무늬

Meaning in Konglish:

A brown trench coat that resembles the style of a Burberry trench coat. It's a popular coat style but not necessarily Burberry brand. It doesn't need to have the classic Burberry design either, so basically a brown trench coat.

Example Konglish Sentence:

I love her _Burberry_.

Translated to American English:

I love her _trench coat_.

Combi-style 콤비 스타일

Meaning in Konglish:

The style when a man wears nice slacks with a different colored blazer or jacket. This can be the same as business casual but refers to the fact that the clothing items are different colors. For example, wearing navy slacks with a gray jacket.

Example Konglish Sentence:

What should we wear to the party? _Combi-style_ is good.

Translated to American English:

What should we wear to the party? _Slacks and a jacket_ is good.

Couple Look 커플룩

Meaning in Konglish:

When a couple matches their clothes, outfits, and all-around look. This is quite common for young couples in Korea.

Example Konglish Sentence:

Oh cute! I like their _couple look_!

Translated to American English:

Oh cute! They are _matching_! I like it!

Oh cute! I like their _matching outfits_!

FREE SIZE 프리 사이즈

Meaning in Konglish:

One size fits all

Example Konglish Sentence:

These *one pieces* are *free size*.

Translated to American English:

These *dresses* are *one size fits all*.

Free Size Dresses

One time, I was shopping in Hawaii at a swap meet or market while on vacation. I came across a little shop with cute dresses. I loved the designs. I asked the owner, who was Korean, "What sizes do you have in these?"

"Free size," he answered. Confused, I looked at my husband expecting him to know. He's Hawaiian. I thought maybe it was a Hawaiian phrase, but he didn't know either.

"Only one size," the shop owner said, "One size for everybody." I understood. He meant "one size fits all."

The next week, a Korean student said the same phrase, "free size." This time, I knew what it meant.

DRESS 드레스

Meaning in Konglish:

Only a formal dress like a wedding dress or evening gown, not everyday dresses

Example Konglish Sentence:

You shouldn't wear a _dress_ to a casual restaurant.

Translated to American English:

You shouldn't wear a _formal dress_ to a casual restaurant.

GOLDEN PANTS / CORDON PANTS 골덴바지

Meaning in Konglish:

Corduroy pants

Example Konglish Sentence:

Golden pants are coming back into style.

Cordon pants are coming back into style.

Translated to American English:

Corduroy pants are coming back into style.

Gown 가운

Meaning in Konglish:

1. A robe worn at home or out of the shower

2. A doctor's white coat or lab coat

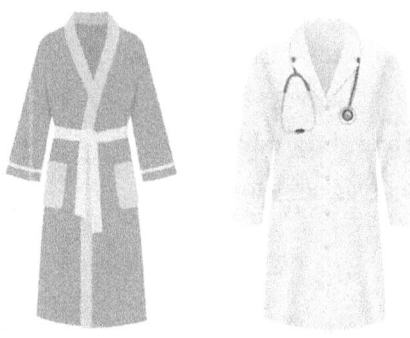

Example Konglish Sentence:

The doctor looked professional in her _gown_.

He always wears a _gown_ at home on the weekends.

Translated to American English:

The doctor looked professional in her _white coat_.

He always wears a _robe_ at home on the weekends.

HALF COAT 하프코트

Meaning in Konglish:

A waist-length coat

Example Konglish Sentence:

I got a new _half coat_ for the winter.

Translated to American English:

I got a new _coat_ for the winter.

JACKU 자크

Meaning in Konglish:

Zipper

Example Konglish Sentence:

My _jacku_ is broken.

Translated to American English:

My _zipper_ is broken.

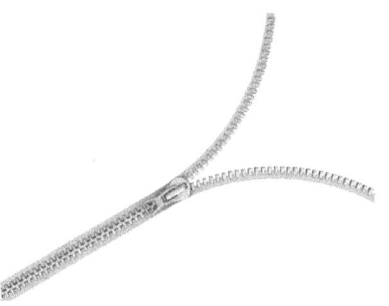

JUMPER 점퍼

Meaning in Konglish:

A general jacket or puffer jacket

Example Konglish Sentence:

I like your *jumper*. Where did you get it?

Translated to American English:

I like your *jacket*. Where did you get it?

SCHOOL JUMPER 학교 점퍼

Meaning in Konglish:

A jacket styled like a letterman jacket

Example Konglish Sentence:

The high school students were all wearing their *school jumpers* at the party.

Translated to American English:

The high school students were all wearing their *letter jackets* at the party.

MUFFLER 머플러

Meaning in Konglish:

A winter scarf

Example Konglish Sentence:

I'm going to give her a _muffler_ for her birthday.

Translated to American English:

I'm going to give her a _scarf_ for her birthday.

Muffler in the Mail

In college, I had a great Korean friend. One year, for my birthday, she told me that she had asked her mom to mail me a special gift from Korea, but it hadn't arrived on time. She said she couldn't find the style in the U.S. that she liked, so she had her mom pick out a muffler for me from Korea. I smiled and thanked her for her kind thought and reassured her that I didn't mind waiting for it to arrive.

When I thought about it later that evening, all I could think was, "What is a muffler?" The only kind of muffler I knew about was the kind that is in your car. I wasn't even totally sure what _that_ muffler was. I just knew that you didn't want it to break. Obviously, she wasn't mailing me a car part for my birthday. Maybe it was a special kind of Korean mittens for the winter?

Later when the gift arrived, I opened the box and found a beautiful winter scarf.

ONE PIECE 원피스

Meaning in Konglish:

A casual dress

Example Konglish Sentence:

She's wearing a *one piece* to the party.

Translated to American English:

She's wearing a *dress* to the party.

What Kind of Party?

Here is a conversation I once had with a Korean student:

Me – What are you going to wear to the party tomorrow?

Student – I'm going to wear a one piece.

Me – Oh? It's a swimming party?

Student *(confused)* – No. It's not a swimming party.

Me *(confused)* – It's not? Then why are you wearing a swimsuit if it's not a swimming party?

Student *(more confused)* – I'm not wearing a swimsuit tomorrow!

Me *(even more confused)* – What? I'm confused. You said you were wearing a one piece tomorrow?

PANTY 팬티

Meaning in Konglish:

Underwear for both men and women

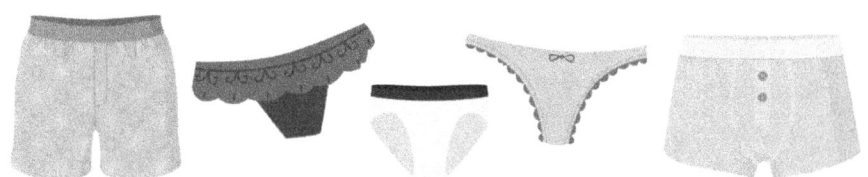

Example Konglish Sentence:

This is my husband's _panty_.

Translated to American English:

These are my husband's _underwear_.

PANTY STOCKINGS 팬티 스타킹

Meaning in Konglish:

Pantyhose

Example Konglish Sentence:

In the USA, *panty stockings* were commonplace in the 1980s, but now they are much less popular.

Translated to American English:

In the USA, *pantyhose*/*stockings* were commonplace in the 1980s, but now they are much less popular.

PADDING 패딩

Meaning in Konglish:

A puffy jacket, puffer jacket, down jacket

Example Konglish Sentence:

I'm surprised that people here are wearing *Burberrys*. In Korea, we usually wear *paddings* in this weather.

Translated to American English:

I'm surprised that people here are wearing *trench coats*. In Korea, we usually wear *puffy jackets* / *down jackets* in this weather.

POLAR T 폴라티

Meaning in Konglish:

Turtleneck shirt/sweater

Example Konglish Sentence:

Some people think _polar t's_ are
fashionable, but others don't agree.

Translated to American English:

Some people think _turtlenecks_ are
fashionable, but others don't agree.

S SIZE

Meaning in Konglish:

Small

Example Konglish Sentence:

She wears _S size_.

Translated to American English:

She wears a _small_.

M SIZE

Meaning in Konglish:

Medium

Example Konglish Sentence:

I need _M size_ shirt.

Translated to American English:

I need a _medium_ shirt.

L SIZE

Meaning in Konglish:

Large

Example Konglish Sentence:

Can you buy an _L size_ for my dad?

Translated to American English:

Can you buy a _large_ for my dad?

LL Size / 2L

Meaning in Konglish:

Extra Large (XL)

Example Konglish Sentence:

Do you sell this shirt in _LL size_?

Translated to American English:

Do you sell this shirt in _extra large_?

LLL Size / 3L

Meaning in Konglish:

Extra extra large (2XL) (XXL)

Example Konglish Sentence:

His shirt size is _LLL_/_3L_.

Translated to American English:

His shirt size is _2XL_.

SEPARATE CODI 세퍼레이트 코디

Meaning in Konglish:

This is similar to combi-style, where you mix and match items of different colors (like navy slacks with a gray jacket), but *separate codi* often includes a combination of three or more colors (rather than two like combi-style).

Example Konglish Sentence:

Spring is the season where people love to do <u>*separate codi*</u> with vibrant colors.

Translated to American English:

Spring is the season where many people love to <u>*mix and match vibrant colors and styles*</u>.

SINGLE STYLE SUIT 수트

Meaning in Konglish:

A suit

Example Konglish Sentence:

He usually wears a <u>*single style suit*</u> to the office.

Translated to American English:

He usually wears a <u>*suit*</u> to the office.

SLIPPERS 슬리퍼

Meaning in Konglish:

Slides or sandals for the bathroom or living room. Most Korean homes have a separate pair of slides/sandals that you only wear in the bathroom, so a Korean host might ask you to wear the "slippers" only in the bathroom.

Example Konglish Sentence:

Please wear these _slippers_ in the bathroom.

Translated to American English:

Please wear these _sandals_/_slides_ in the bathroom.

Korean Life & Culture – Bathroom Slippers

As you may already know, it is customary to take off your shoes when entering a Korean home. Most houses have an entry area near the front door, called a _hyeongwan_, where you can leave your shoes. You'll walk around the house barefooted or with socks or slippers, but there is one important exception. When you enter the bathroom, you should be prepared to put on a special pair of bathroom _slippers_. These are usually rubber, athletic-style slides that are worn only in the bathroom. This will help keep your feet clean while on the potentially dirty bathroom floor, and it will prevent you from from tracking bathroom grime into the rest of the house.

TRAINING (BOK) 트레이닝복

Meaning in Konglish:

Similar to a sweatsuit but thinner like a tracksuit or athletic wear

Example Konglish Sentence:

I like her new _training_.

Translated to American English:

I like her new _track suit_.

TWO PIECE 투피스

Meaning in Konglish:

A women's suit, pantsuit, skirt suit

Example Konglish Sentence:

She wore a _two piece_ to the office for her first day of work at the new job.

Translated to American English:

She wore a _skirt suit_ / _pantsuit_ for her first day of work at the new job.

WALKER 워커

Meaning in Konglish:

Heavy military style or combat style boots
with a thick sole

Example Konglish Sentence:

He has cool _walkers_.

Translated to American English:

He has cool _boots_ / _combat (style) boots_.

Y SHIRT 와이 셔츠

Meaning in Konglish:

White button-up dress shirts that men in Korea
usually wear to work

Example Konglish Sentence:

I can't find my _Y shirt_. I need it for work
tomorrow.

Translated to American English:

I can't find my _white button-up shirt_.
I can't find my _white dress shirt_.
I need it for work tomorrow.

ACCESSORIES

Scan for Audio

CROSS BAG 크로스백

Meaning in Konglish:

Crossbody bag

Example Konglish Sentence:

I love her _cross bag_.

Translated to American English:

I love her _crossbody (bag)_.

HAIR BAND 헤어 밴드

Meaning in Konglish:

Headband or sweatband

Example Konglish Sentence:

I want to buy that _hair band_ for my sister.

Translated to American English:

I want to buy that _headband_ for my sister.

HAIR PIN 헤어 핀

Meaning in Konglish:

Hair clip, bobby pin, barrette

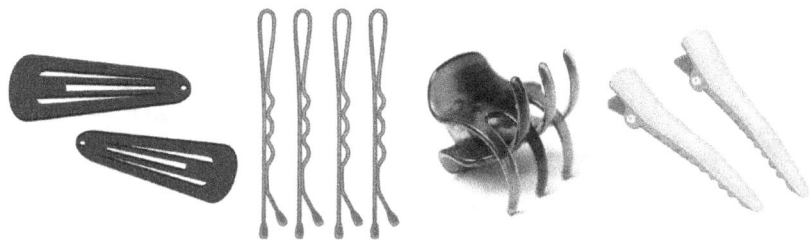

Example Konglish Sentence:

Your _hair pin_ is so cool.

Translated to American English:

Your _hair clip_ is so cool.

I love your _hair clip_.

MANICURE 매니큐어

Meaning in Konglish:

Nail polish

Example Konglish Sentence:

I like your _manicure_ color a lot.

Your _manicure_ color is so nice.

Translated to American English:

I like your _nail polish_ a lot.

I love that _nail (polish)_ color.

RIBBON 리본

Meaning in Konglish:

1. Bow
2. Bow tie

Example Konglish Sentence:

The pink _ribbon_ in that baby's hair is so cute.
The men had good-looking _ribbons_ at the
wedding.

Translated to American English:

The pink _bow_ in that baby's hair is so cute.
The men had good-looking _bow ties_ at the wedding.

SACK 쌕

Meaning in Konglish:

Fanny pack, crossbody fanny pack,
or small backpack

Example Konglish Sentence:

I bought a cute orange _sack_ to go with this
dress.

Translated to American English:

I bought a cute orange _fanny pack_ to go with this dress.

5

MAKEUP AND SKINCARE

Scan for Audio

CUSHION 쿠션

Meaning in Konglish:

A popular kind of Korean wet dry
foundation, sometimes sold in the U.S. as
"Korean cushion foundation"

Example Konglish Sentence:

I need to buy a new _cushion_.
The _maker_ I liked discontinued the product.

Translated to American English:

I need to buy a new _Korean cushion foundation_ / _wet dry foundation_ for my face.
The _brand_ I liked discontinued the product.

EYE REMOVER 아이 리무버

Meaning in Konglish:

Makeup remover

Example Konglish Sentence:

I usually use _eye remover_ at night to take off my makeup.

Translated to American English:

I usually use _(eye) makeup remover_ at night to take off my makeup.

PACK 팩

Meaning in Konglish:

1. To wrap (gifts)

2. Skincare mask, facial mask, face mask

3. Sandwich bag

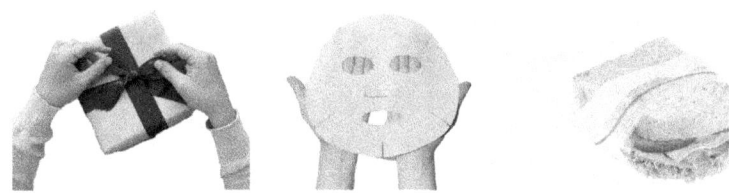

Example Konglish Sentence:

Let's _pack_ all the Christmas presents!

Korea is famous for its rejuvenating _packs_.

Let's put the fruit in a _pack_.

Translated to American English:

Let's _wrap_ all the Christmas presents!

Korea is famous for its rejuvenating _facial masks_.

Let's put the fruit in a _sandwich bag_.

Rinse 린스

Meaning in Konglish:

Conditioner

Example Konglish Sentence:

Some people don't use _rinse_ for their hair.

Translated to American English:

Some people don't use _conditioner_ for their hair.

Rouge 루즈

Meaning in Konglish:

Lipstick

Example Konglish Sentence:

I love your _rouge_ color.

Translated to American English:

I love your _lip color_. I love your _lipstick_ color.

SKIN 스킨

Meaning in Konglish:

Skin toner

Example Konglish Sentence:

My mother told me I should always use _skin_ on my face at night.

Translated to American English:

My mother told me I should always use _toner_ on my face at night.

BODY AND PHYSICAL APPEARANCE

Scan for Audio

BODYLINE 바디라인

Meaning in Konglish:

The shape of your body, your figure

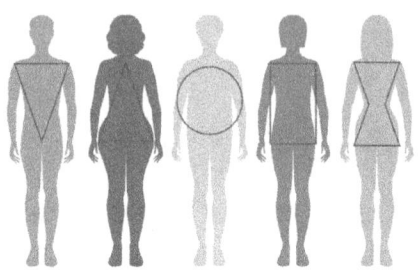

Example Konglish Sentence:

She has a good _bodyline_.

I need to exercise to improve my _bodyline_.

Translated to American English:

She has a good _figure_.

I need to exercise to improve my _figure_.

DOUBLE EYELID 쌍커풀

Meaning in Konglish:

The upper eyelid crease or fold in your eyelid that creates definition between your eyelid and above your eyelid; the shape of a typical Caucasian eyelid

Example Konglish Sentence:

I want to have *double eyelid* like Caucasian people.

Translated to American English:

I want to have a *crease in my eyelid* like Caucasian people.

Korean Life & Culture – Double Eyelid Surgery

Plastic surgery is extremely common in South Korea. In fact, there is a popular plastic surgery called *double eyelid surgery*, where patients can widen their eyes to look bigger and more defined. In American plastic surgery, you may hear this procedure called blepharoplasty, (Asian) eyelid surgery, or eyelid crease surgery, though *double eyelid surgery* is catching on. I had a few Korean friends in college who had "double eyelid surgery." When they first told me, I had a hard time understanding. Double eyelids? They didn't seem to have any extra eyelids. I couldn't imagine what they might mean. My friends were patient and explained the procedure and the phrasing.

As an example of Konglish confusion, years ago, a good friend of mine used to work as a hospital translator at a famous Korean hospital. Many Asian-Americans would come to this hospital to get this eye-widening surgery to create more defined eyelids. My friend translated into English, "You are here for your double eyelid surgery." More than once, her American patients didn't know what she was talking about and felt afraid that maybe they had been scheduled for the wrong surgery.

GLAMOUR 글래머

Meaning in Konglish:

A curvy, voluptuous woman

Example Konglish Sentence:

People love _glamour_ women nowadays.

Translated to American English:

People love _curvy_ women nowadays.

HIP 힙

Meaning in Konglish:

Hips and buttocks

Example Konglish Sentence:

She has a big _hip_.

The doctor gave me a shot in my _hip_.

Translated to American English:

She has a big _butt_.

The doctor gave me a shot in my _buttocks_.

LOSE MY/YOUR WEIGHT

Meaning in Konglish:

Lose weight

Example Konglish Sentence:

Did you *lose your weight*? You look thin.

Translated to American English:

Did you *lose weight*? You look thin.

Korean Life & Culture – Discussing Weight

In Korean culture, it is much more acceptable to mention or comment on weight than it is in American culture. "Did you lose weight? You look thin," or "You look healthy" (often code for "you gained weight") are common greetings or comments in both social life and the workplace and are not considered offensive. Even more direct comments like, "You should eat less bacon," or "He is very fat," can sometimes be expected. While such comments about weight and body are certainly an annoyance even to many young Koreans, they are not considered highly offensive or taboo as they would be in the United States.

IMAGE 이미지

Meaning in Konglish:

Reputation, public image

Example Konglish Sentence:

Her _image_ is not nice.

Translated to American English:

She doesn't have a very good _reputation_.

OUTLOOK 아웃룩

Meaning in Konglish:

Physical appearance

Example Konglish Sentence:

Her _outlook_ is bad today. Did she even take a shower?

You shouldn't judge someone by only their _outlook_.

Translated to American English:

She _looks_ bad today. Did she even take a shower?

You shouldn't judge someone by only their _appearance_.

S-LINE 에스라인

Meaning in Konglish:

Hourglass figure

Example Konglish Sentence:

She has a perfect _S-line_.

Translated to American English:

She has an _hourglass figure_.

V-LINE 브이라인

Meaning in Konglish:

A V-shaped face with thin cheeks and a pointed chin. This is a very desirable look in Korea, and there is a popular plastic surgery to help create this look and shape in one's face.

Example Konglish Sentence:

Many Korean celebrities have plastic surgery to get a _V-line_.

Translated to American English:

Many Korean celebrities have plastic surgery to get _thinner cheeks and a pointed chin_.

VISUAL 비주얼

Meaning in Konglish:

Appearance, looks

Example Konglish Sentence:

His _visual_ is so good today.

You shouldn't judge people by only their _visual_.

Translated to American English:

He _looks_ so good today.

You shouldn't judge people by only their _appearance_/_looks_.

7

HEALTH

Scan for Audio

BALANCED MEAL 균형잡힌 식단

Meaning in Konglish:

A balanced diet

Example Konglish Sentence:

A *balanced meal* is good for health.

Translated to American English:

A *balanced diet* is good for you.

BAND 밴드

Meaning in Konglish:

Band-Aid

Example Konglish Sentence:

Your cut is bleeding.

Do you need a *band*?

He has a big *band*.

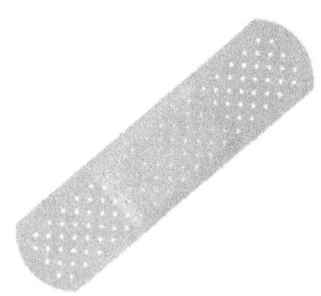

Translated to American English:

Your cut is bleeding.

Do you need a *Band-Aid*?

He has a big *Band-Aid*.

CONDITION 컨디션

Meaning in Konglish:

Your health or current feeling

Example Konglish Sentence:

What's your _condition_? My _condition_ today is not good.

I feel so tired now, and I'm not sure if I can make it today. I can tell you in one hour. I think I need to see my _condition_.

We don't know our _body condition_, so we should be careful going out if others have a contagious disease.

Translated to American English:

How do you _feel_ today? I don't _feel very well_ today. I'm _feeling_ a bit under the weather today.

I feel so tired now, and I'm not sure if I can make it today. I can tell you in one hour. I think I need to see _how I'm feeling_ in a little while.

We don't know _how well our immune system is working_, so we should be careful going out if others have a contagious disease.

CHECK UP 첵업

Meaning in Konglish:

This is not a true Konglish term but is commonly heard when speaking English with Koreans. *Check up* is commonly used as a verb, rather than a noun, for an annual doctor's appointment.

Example Konglish Sentence:

I _checked up_ when I was in Korea because it's much cheaper to visit a doctor there.

Translated to American English:

I _got a checkup_ when I was in Korea because it's much cheaper to go to the doctor there.

DIET 다이어트

Meaning in Konglish:

This refers to the whole process of losing weight, including diet and exercise.

Example Konglish Sentence:

I am going to the gym because I am on a _diet_.

Translated to American English:

I am going to the gym because I'm _trying to lose weight_. I'm trying to get in shape.

DISK 디스크

Meaning in Konglish:

Slipped disk, herniated disk, ruptured disk

Example Konglish Sentence:

She hurt her back.

She has a _disk_.

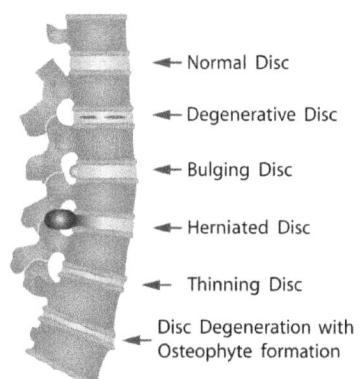

- Normal Disc
- Degenerative Disc
- Bulging Disc
- Herniated Disc
- Thinning Disc
- Disc Degeneration with Osteophyte formation

Translated to American English:

She hurt her back.

She has a _slipped disk_ / _herniated disk_.

The Injury

A student once told me, "I can't come to class this week because I have a disk." I was very confused. A disk? A DVD? A desk? A frisbee? I couldn't understand why he would need to miss one week of class for any reasons I could fathom related to "a disk."

I saw his wife the next day, and when I asked about her weekend, she said, "It was terrible! We had to go to the hospital. My husband has a disk."

Still confused, I realized _disk_ might mean something medical, so I asked more questions. She told me her husband had hurt his back, and I finally understood that she meant he had a "slipped disk" or "herniated disk."

FITNESS 헬스장

Meaning in Konglish:

A gym or place to exercise and work out

Example Konglish Sentence:

He works at a _fitness_, so he can exercise for free any time.

Translated to American English:

He works at a _gym_, so he can exercise for free any time.

GARGLE 가글

Meaning in Konglish:

Mouthwash

Example Konglish Sentence:

I need to buy some _gargle_.

I use _gargle_ every day.

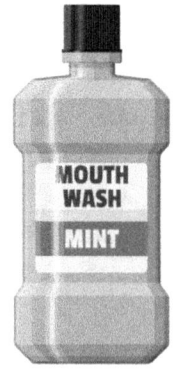

Translated to American English:

I need to buy some _mouthwash_.

I use _mouthwash_ every day.

Gyps 깁스

Meaning in Konglish:

A cast for when you break a bone

Example Konglish Sentence:

She broke her leg, and now she has a _gyps_.

Translated to American English:

She broke her leg, and now she has a _cast_.

Healing Time 힐링타임

Meaning in Konglish:

Self-care, rest, and relaxation

Example Konglish Sentence:

I like to have a _healing time_ at a spa.

Translated to American English:

I like to _relax_ at a spa. It's my _self-care_.

HEALTH 헬스

Meaning in Konglish:

A gym or place to exercise and work out

Example Konglish Sentence:

He works at a _health_, so he can work out for free anytime.

Translated to American English:

He works at a _gym_, so he can work out for free anytime.

HEALTHY MEAL 건강한 식사

Meaning in Konglish:

A healthy diet

Example Konglish Sentence:

He has diabetes, so his doctor told him to start eating a _healthy meal_.

Translated to American English:

He has diabetes, so his doctor told him to start eating a _healthy diet_.

HOSPITAL 호스피탈

Meaning in Konglish:

Hospital, doctor's office, clinic

Example Konglish Sentence:

- Can we reschedule today's class? I need to take my son to the _hospital_.
- Oh my gosh! Is he OK?! Do you need anything?!

Translated to American English:

- Can we reschedule today's class? My son has a _doctor's appointment_.
- Sure, no problem. See you next week.

OMG! Are you OK?!

Over the years, I've had many students from private English lessons text me with things like, "I'm sorry, I need to cancel the lesson today. I need to go to the hospital," or, "I am going to the hospital with my son, so I need to reschedule our class." The first time I received a text like this, I understandably responded with, "Are you OK?! Do you need anything? Can I bring you anything? Please let me know if there's anything you need!!!" In most cases, I found out that the student was simply going to a scheduled appointment or a typical doctor's appointment for a child who woke up with a slight fever.

MR 엠알

Meaning in Konglish:

MRI

Example Konglish Sentence:

Yun broke her leg and needed an _MR_.

Translated to American English:

Yun broke her leg and needed an _MRI_.

OVEREAT 오바이트

Meaning in Konglish:

To vomit or throw up

Example Konglish Sentence:

I drank too much yesterday, so I _overate_.

I drank too much yesterday, so I did _overeat_.

Translated to American English:

I drank too much yesterday, so I _threw up_.

PASS 파스

Meaning in Konglish:

A popular medicated pain patch used for bruises, aches, sore muscles, and other similar conditions

Example Konglish Sentence:

I got a bad bruise, so my grandma gave me a _pass_.

Translated to American English:

I got a bad bruise, so my grandma gave me a _pain patch_.

PAY DOCTOR 페이닥터

Meaning in Konglish:

This is a doctor who doesn't have his or her own practice and works for a hospital or another boss.

Example Konglish Sentence:

He works at the hospital. He is a _pay doctor_.

Translated to American English:

He works at the hospital. He is a _doctor_.

RINGER 링거/링겔

Meaning in Konglish:

An IV or IV fluids

Example Konglish Sentence:

He got a _ringer_ at the hospital.

Translated to American English:

He got _IV fluids_ at the hospital.

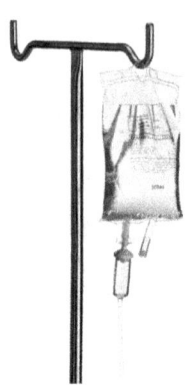

SUNCREAM 선크림

Meaning in Konglish:

Sunscreen, sunblock

Example Konglish Sentence:

You should use _suncream_ every day.

Translated to American English:

You should use _sunscreen_ every day.

WELL BEING 웰빙

Meaning in Konglish:

Healthy or good for you

Example Konglish Sentence:

This spinach is _well being_.

Translated to American English:

This spinach is _healthy_.

SCHOOL, WORK, AND AROUND THE OFFICE

ACADEMIC CLASS 아카데믹 클래스

Meaning in Konglish:

Usually an extra class taken at an after-school tutoring center (called a *hagwon* in Korea), not a class taken in school

Example Konglish Sentence:

He has many *academic classes*.

Translated to American English:

He has many *extra classes after school at the tutoring center*.

Korean Life & Culture – Hagwons & Tutoring Culture

In Korea, you will find that it is extremely common for students of all ages, especially middle school and high school students, to attend *hagwons* or private tutoring centers after school each day. Sometimes in the United States, tutoring can suggest that one is behind and needs extra help to catch up with the rest of his or her grade level. However, in Korea, tutoring or attending a *hagwon* has no such connotation. Education in Korea is highly competitive, and most students with the financial means, whether A-students or F-students, attend *hagwons* for everything from preparing for college entrance exams to learning more in depth material of a single subject all the way to exploring extracurricular activities like learning a musical instrument or playing a sport. *Hagwons* are also popular for studying foreign languages like English. While not all modern parents are fans of this *hagwon* culture for their kids, *hagwons* are often considered essential to one's academic success, even more important than school itself. So don't be surprised if you meet students who attend school until 4 or 5pm, then go directly to a *hagwon* where they study until 10 or 11pm or maybe even midnight.

ACADEMY 학원

Meaning in Konglish:

Usually a *hagwon*, an after-school tutoring center that offers extra classes, both academic and extracurricular (math, piano, soccer, etc.)

Example Konglish Sentence:

He studies math at the _academy_.

Translated to American English:

He studies math at the _after-school tutoring center_.
He studies math at the _Korean hagwon_.

BALL PEN 볼펜

Meaning in Konglish:

A ball point pen

Example Konglish Sentence:

Do you have a _ball pen_ I can borrow?

Translated to American English:

Do you have a _pen_ I can borrow?

BLUE WORKER 블루 워커

Meaning in Konglish:

Blue-collar worker

Example Konglish Sentence:

That city has a lot of _blue workers_.

Translated to American English:

That city has a lot of _blue-collar workers_.

BOND 본드

Meaning in Konglish:

Strong glue or superglue

Example Konglish Sentence:

Where did you get that _bond_?

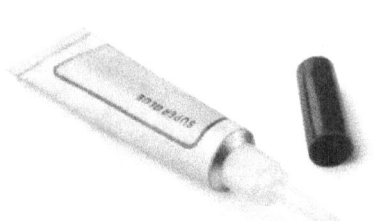

Translated to American English:

Where did you get that _(super)glue_?

CIRCLE 써클/동아리

Meaning in Konglish:

Club at school or in college

Example Konglish Sentence:

I was in the soccer _circle_ when I was in university.

Translated to American English:

I was in the soccer _club_ when I was in college.

CLIP 클립

Meaning in Konglish:

Paperclip

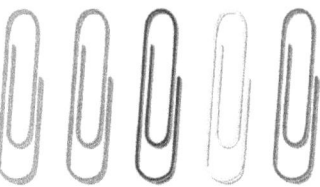

Example Konglish Sentence:

Please use a _clip_ to attach your check to your application.

Translated to American English:

Please use a _paperclip_ to attach your check to your application.

COURSE 코스

Meaning in Konglish:

Program, major, or class

Example Konglish Sentence:

I took the English _course_ at university.

Translated to American English:

I _majored in_ English in college.

I took an English _class_ in college.

CUNNING 컨닝

Meaning in Konglish:

Cheating on a test

Example Konglish Sentence:

"Teacher, he's _cunning_ me!"

Translated to American English:

"He's _cheating_!"

"He's _cheating_ off of me!"

"He's _cheating_ on the test!"

DIARY 다이어리

Meaning in Konglish:

Planner with your schedule in it

Example Konglish Sentence:

May 15? That might be good. Let me check my _diary_ to see if I have a _schedule._

Translated to American English:

May 15? That might be good. Let me check my _planner_ to see if I have any _plans._

ENGINEER 엔진이어

Meaning in Konglish:

A technician or skilled worker who can fix technical or mechanical types of problems, for example, an electrician, an IT worker, a plumber, a car mechanic. It can include engineers as Americans think of them, but it doesn't necessarily have to be a person with a college degree in engineering.

Example Konglish Sentence:

My husband is an _engineer._

Translated to American English:

My husband is a _repairman_/_technician._

HARD BOARD 하드 보드

Meaning in Konglish:

Poster board

Example Konglish Sentence:

My son needs some _hard board_ for his school project.

Translated to American English:

My son needs some _poster board_ for his school project.

HOTCHKISS 호치키스

Meaning in Konglish:

Stapler

Example Konglish Sentence:

Wow, I can't believe your _Hotchkiss_ is made of gold.

Translated to American English:

Wow, I can't believe your _stapler_ is made of gold.

JUNIOR 후배

Meaning in Konglish:

1. Someone younger than you
2. Someone who has worked at your company for a shorter period of time in a lower position (which usually means they are younger than you in Korea)

Example Konglish Sentence:

I met my *junior* at a market.

Translated to American English:

I ran into a girl I went to high school with at a market. She was *a grade younger than me / a grade behind me*.

Korean Life & Culture – Age Hierarchy

In South Korea, it is very common to talk about age. "How old are you?" is a common question for someone you are meeting for the first time. Your age commonly determines your position in a job, so even in the workplace, this is a normal topic of discussion. The Korean language has different levels of respect and formality, many of which are determined by age. If you are speaking to someone older than you, even just one year older, you will likely speak to them using different word forms than you would if speaking to someone the same age or younger than you. So culturally, even when speaking English, talking about age in Korea is not considered taboo for adults as it sometimes is in the United States.

LETTERING 레터링

Meaning in Konglish:

Handwriting

Example Konglish Sentence:

He has elegant *lettering*.

Translated to American English:

He has elegant *handwriting*.

MAGIC 매직

Meaning in Konglish:

Magic marker, permanent marker, Sharpie

Example Konglish Sentence:

I'd like to write this with a *magic*.

Translated to American English:

I'd like to write this with a *permanent marker*.

NAME PEN 네임펜

Meaning in Konglish:

A thin felt-tipped permanent marker often used for signing things, a thin-tipped Sharpie

Example Konglish Sentence:

Please put your *sign* here with your *name pen*.

Translated to American English:

Please put your *signature* here with a *Sharpie*.

NAME CARD 네임 카드

Meaning in Konglish:

Business card

Example Konglish Sentence:

It's nice to meet you. Do you have a *name card*?

Translated to American English:

It's nice to meet you. Do you have a *business card*?

NOTE 노트

Meaning in Konglish:

Notebook or notecard

Example Konglish Sentence:

Let me write this in my _note_.

Translated to American English:

Let me write this in my _notebook_.

NOTEBOOK 노트북

Meaning in Konglish:

Laptop computer

Example Konglish Sentence:

Let me type this in my _notebook_.

Translated to American English:

Let me type this in my _computer_/_laptop_.

OFFICER 오피서

Meaning in Konglish:

Anyone with a government job; federal worker, federal employee, public servant, and anyone who works for a government-associated company. These are typically well-respected jobs that require passing difficult exams to even be considered for a position.

Example Konglish Sentence:

My son is an _officer_.

Translated to American English:

My son is a _government worker_ / _federal worker_ / _works for the government_.

The Officer

I once had a student from South Korea who told me her son was an "officer." For months, I thought her son was a police officer or perhaps even a ranked military officer in Korea. At one point, we were talking about him, and I asked, "Is it dangerous to be an officer in Korea?" She looked really confused, maybe even offended, "Of course not." I later found out that he worked for a government agency in the finance department and that _officer_ did not mean the same thing to Koreans as it did to me.

ONE BY ONE 원 바이 원

Meaning in Konglish:

One on one, private

Example Konglish Sentence:

I'd like to take a lesson _one by one_.

Let's have a conversation _one by one_.

Translated to American English:

I'd like to take a _one on one_ / _private_ lesson.

Let's have a conversation _one on one_ / _in private_.

PRINT 프린트

Meaning in Konglish:

A handout or printout

Example Konglish Sentence:

He brought _prints_ for everyone at the meeting.

Translated to American English:

He brought _handouts_ for everyone at the meeting.

He brought _print outs_ for everyone at the meeting.

READ LOUD 리드아웃

Meaning in Konglish:

Read out loud, aloud

Example Konglish Sentence:

We're going to _read this chapter loud_.

Translated to American English:

We're going to _read this chapter out loud_.

We're going to _read this chapter aloud_.

SALARYMAN 샐러리맨

Meaning in Konglish:

Anyone who receives an annual salary payment from working as an employee under a boss. They do not own their own business. This is usually used for full-time, salaried workers of non-exec jobs.

Example Konglish Sentence:

Her dad is a _salaryman_.

Translated to American English:

Her dad _works at XYZ company_.

SENIOR 선배

Meaning in Konglish:

1. Someone older than you
2. Someone in a higher position than you at work or school (which usually means they are older than you)

Example Konglish Sentence:

One of my *seniors* in college was very mean.

Translated to American English:

This guy, who was *a year ahead of me* in college, was very mean.

He was *a year ahead of me* in college, and he was very mean.

Korean Life & Culture – Korean Age

There is an important difference in how Koreans and Americans calculate age. When I first visited South Korea, I was 20 years old. My friend introduced me to one of her cousins who seemed a lot younger than us, but he said he was 16. When he told me he was in middle school, I was even more confused. Finally, I asked my friend about this, and she started laughing when she realized the mix-up. He was 16 in KOREAN age but only 14 in international (American) age. She also informed me that I was 22 in Korean age. I was shocked! I had no idea that two different systems for calculating age even existed! Koreans already know that most other countries do not use the same system, but if someone asks about your age, it may be a good idea to clarify whether it's your Korean age or international age.

Calculating Age in Korea

Here's how it works: When you are born, you count yourself as 1 year old. Then you turn a new age at the beginning of each new year. So beware that depending on your date of birth, your age can vary anywhere from 1 day to 2 years different from your international age.

Here are a few examples:

Example 1:

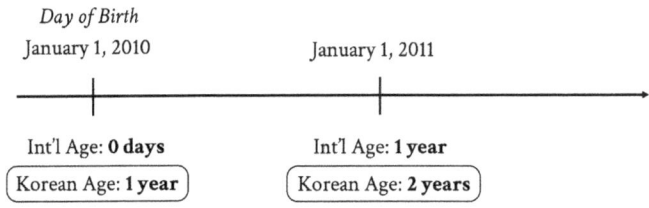

Example 2:

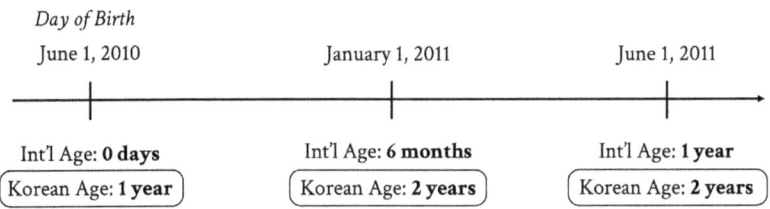

Example 3:

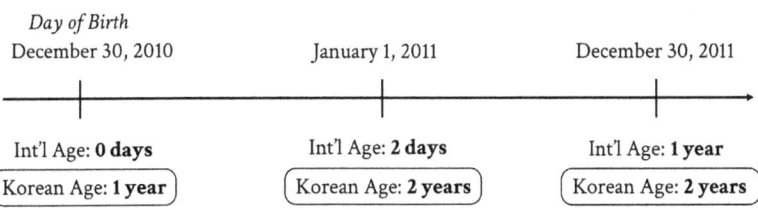

*Note: As of 2023, the law in South Korea has changed and "Korean age" is no longer used in an official capacity.

SHARP 샤프

Meaning in Konglish:

Mechanical pencil

Example Konglish Sentence:

Let's write this with a _sharp_.

Translated to American English:

Let's write this with a _mechanical pencil_.

SIGN PEN 싸인펜

Meaning in Konglish:

A thin felt-tipped permanent marker
often used for signing things

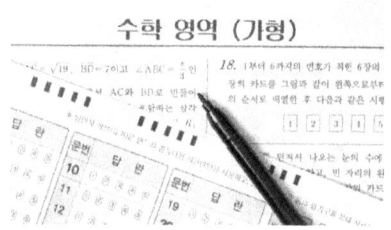

Example Konglish Sentence:

Please put your _sign_ here with your
sign pen.

Translated to American English:

Please put your _signature_ here with a _felt-tipped pen_.

SPECS 스펙

Meaning in Konglish:

Qualifications and experience like on a resume

Example Konglish Sentence:

The candidate for the job has some very good _specs_.

Translated to American English:

The candidate for the job has some very good _qualifications and experience_.

TRAINING 트레이닝

Meaning in Konglish:

An internship or long training period

Example Konglish Sentence:

He's doing a _training_ with XYZ company this summer.

Translated to American English:

He's doing an _internship_ with XYZ company this summer.

WHITE 화이트

Meaning in Konglish:

White out

Example Konglish Sentence:

I made a mistake. I need some _white_.

Translated to American English:

I made a mistake. I need some _white out_.

WHITE WORKER 화이트워커

Meaning in Konglish:

White-collar worker

Example Konglish Sentence:

He was a _white worker_ for 20 years, so he was excited for a change when he retired and started learning to be a mechanic.

Translated to American English:

He was a _white-collar worker_ for 20 years, so he was excited for a change when he retired and started learning to be a mechanic.

WORKING LEVEL PEOPLE 직원/사원

Meaning in Konglish:

Non-execs or people in a company who don't have executive positions

Example Konglish Sentence:

A lot of _working level people_ in Korea work at night as well as during the day.

Translated to American English:

A lot of _non-execs_ in Korea feel pressured to work late hours.

9

TECHNOLOGY

Scan for Audio

COMPUTER 컴퓨터

Meaning in Konglish:

Desktop computer

Example Konglish Sentence:

I don't have a _computer_; I only have a laptop.

Translated to American English:

I don't have a _desktop computer_; I only have a laptop.

DIKA 디카

Meaning in Konglish:

Digital camera

Example Konglish Sentence:

I'm bringing my _dika_ on our trip.

Translated to American English:

I'm bringing my _digital camera_ on our trip.

FLASH 플래시

Meaning in Konglish:

Flashlight

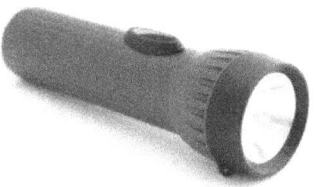

Example Konglish Sentence:

When you go camping, you should always take a _flash_.

Translated to American English:

When you go camping, you should always take a _flashlight_.

GAME ROOM /PC BAR / PC ROOM
게임방/피씨방

Meaning in Konglish:

A place like an internet cafe but for gaming, where people can go to play computer games next to many others

Example Konglish Sentence:

I loved going to the _game room_ / _PC room_ when I was young.

Translated to American English:

I loved going to the _gaming cafe_ to play computer games with my friends when I was young.

GMAP 지 맵

Meaning in Konglish:

Google Maps

Example Konglish Sentence:

I always use _GMap_ so I don't get lost.

Translated to American English:

I always use _Google Maps_ so I don't get lost.

HAND PHONE 핸드 폰

Meaning in Konglish:

Cell phone

Example Konglish Sentence:

I'm shocked that even kids have _hand phones_ nowadays.

Translated to American English:

I'm shocked that even kids have _(cell) phones_ nowadays.

HOMEPI 홈피

Meaning in Konglish:

Website

Example Konglish Sentence:

I found the information on the _homepi_.

Translated to American English:

I found the information on the _website_.

ID / MEMBER ID 아이디

Meaning in Konglish:

Username or Login

Example Konglish Sentence:

What's your _member ID_ for Facebook?

Translated to American English:

What's your _username_ or _login_ for Facebook?

NAVI/NAVIGATION 네비/네비게이션

Meaning in Konglish:

Car GPS, navigation system

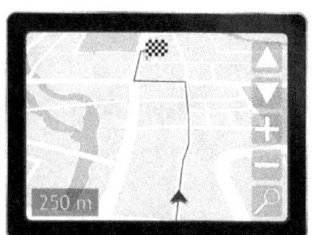

Example Konglish Sentence:

Does your car have _navi_?

Translated to American English:

Does your car have a _GPS_?

PC 피씨

Meaning in Konglish:

Desktop computer

Example Konglish Sentence:

My _PC_ is pretty old, so it does not work well.

Translated to American English:

My _(desktop) computer_ is pretty old, so it does not work well.

SECRET NUMBER 비밀번호

Meaning in Konglish:

Password or PIN number

Example Konglish Sentence:

You should never share your _secret number_.

Translated to American English:

You should never share your _password_ / _pin number_.

SELCA 셀카

Meaning in Konglish:

Selfie

Example Konglish Sentence:

Let's take a _selca_!

Translated to American English:

Let's take a _selfie_!

SELF-CAM 셀프캠

Meaning in Konglish:

1. Taking a video of yourself, a selfie but a video

2. This can also mean the phone stand or phone holder you might use to take a video of yourself

Example Konglish Sentence:

Self-cams are popular for teenagers on social media.

Translated to American English:

It's popular for teenagers to _take and post videos of themselves_ on social media.

10

MONEY

Scan for Audio

Big Money 빅머니

Meaning in Konglish:

A lot of money

Example Konglish Sentence:

The boss makes _big money_.

Translated to American English:

The boss makes _a lot of money_.

Fund 펀드

Meaning in Konglish:

Fundraiser to raise money

Example Konglish Sentence:

They have a _fund_ for the library every year.

Translated to American English:

They have a _fundraiser_ for the library every year.

POCKET MONEY 포켓 머니

Meaning in Konglish:

Spending money, extra money, an allowance

Example Konglish Sentence:

He earned some *pocket money* by selling his old books.

Translated to American English:

He earned some *extra money* by selling his old books.

POOR 포어

Meaning in Konglish:

1. Bad at something or pitiful
2. An expression of feeling sorry for someone

Example Konglish Sentence:

He is so *poor at* basketball.

She broke his heart. He is so *poor*.

Translated to American English:

He is so *bad at* basketball.

She broke his heart. He is so *sad*. / *I feel so bad for him*.

RENTAL FEE 렌트비

Meaning in Konglish:

The amount paid for rent

Example Konglish Sentence:

In the United States, you pay your _rental fee_ for your _apart_ each month.

Translated to American English:

In the United States, you pay your _rent_ for your _apartment_ each month.

SMALL MONEY 스몰 머니

Meaning in Konglish:

A little money, not enough money, or less money

Example Konglish Sentence:

My son wants to become a _gagman_. That's OK, but will he be comfortable making _small money_?

Translated to American English:

My son wants to become a _comedian_. That's OK, but will he be comfortable making such _little money_?

11

SHOPPING

Bargain 바겐

Meaning in Konglish:

A sale

Example Konglish Sentence:

That store is having a _bargain_ this weekend.

Translated to American English:

That store is having a _sale_ this weekend.

Corner 코너

Meaning in Konglish:

Area or department of a store

Example Konglish Sentence:

I went to the fish _corner_ to buy some fish.

Translated to American English:

I went to the seafood _department_ to buy some fish.

DEPART/DEPARTMENT 디파트/디파트먼드

Meaning in Konglish:

A depart is a huge department store that functions similarly to an American shopping mall. It usually has different departments selling different items and even a food court for lunch. Rather than a shopping mall made up of different stores and companies renting space, the depart is all one entity. A Korean depart is similar to a Macy's flagship location (e.g., Macy's Herald Square in New York City). Basically, imagine if a modern Macy's owned the entire mall.

Example Konglish Sentence:

In Korea, you can spend all day at a _depart_! They're so big and have everything!

Translated to American English:

In Korea, you can spend all day at a _department store_! They're so big and have everything!

Doz 다스

Meaning in Konglish:

A dozen

Example Konglish Sentence:

-How many donuts do you want?

- A _doz_.

Translated to American English:

-How many donuts do you want?

-A _dozen_.

EYE SHOPPING 아이 쇼핑

Meaning in Konglish:

Window shopping

Example Konglish Sentence:

I'm not planning to buy anything today, just _eye shopping_.

Translated to American English:

I'm not planning to buy anything today, just _window shopping_.

I'm not planning to buy anything today, just _looking around_.

GROCERY 그로셔리

Meaning in Konglish:

Grocery store

Example Konglish Sentence:

I went to the _grocery_ on Sunday.

Translated to American English:

I went to the _grocery store_ on Sunday.

HANDMADE 핸드메이드

Meaning in Konglish:

Handmade, homemade, made from scratch

Example Konglish Sentence:

Our soup is *handmade*.

Translated to American English:

Our soup is *made from scratch*.

MAKER 메이커

Meaning in Konglish:

Brand

Example Konglish Sentence:

What's the *maker* of these sunglasses?

Translated to American English:

What *brand* are these sunglasses?

MART 마트

Meaning in Konglish:

A big grocery store or supermarket or superstore

Example Konglish Sentence:

I went to the _mart_ this weekend.

Translated to American English:

I went to the _grocery store_ this weekend.

I went to the _supermarket_ this weekend.

ONE PLUS ONE 원플러스원

Meaning in Konglish:

Buy one, get one free sale

Example Konglish Sentence:

The store is having a _one plus one_.

Translated to American English:

The store is having a
buy one, get one free sale.

PART 파트

Meaning in Konglish:

Department (e.g., customer service department)

Example Konglish Sentence:

She works in the accounting _part_.

I didn't like working in the produce _part_ at the mart.

Translated to American English:

She works in the accounting _department_.

I didn't like working in the produce _department_ at the grocery store.

The Fish Part

Recently, I was shopping in the United States at our local Korean store and needed to buy some sweet potatoes. I didn't see any, so as we walked around the story away from the produce department, I kept my eyes opened for any other employees I could ask about it. Finally, we got to the seafood area, and I saw a nice and knowledgeable-looking lady.

"Excuse me, do you have any fresh sweet potatoes today?" I asked.

"I'm sorry, I don't know. This is the fish part," she responded.

"_Gam-sa-hab-ni-da_," I said in my very bad American accent to thank her for her time.

My husband looked slightly confused, but thankfully because my Korean friends and students have taught me tons of Konglish, I understood. We were in the fish department, and if we wanted to know about the sweet potatoes, we would have to ask someone else.

SELF 셀프

Meaning in Konglish:

Self-service, self-serve, BYO

Example Konglish Sentence:

The ice cream is _self_.

The _drinks_ are self.

Translated to American English:

The ice cream is _self-serve_.

Bring your own (BYO) drinks.

SERVICE 서비스

Meaning in Konglish:

Free or complementary items a manager might give customers at a restaurant or store

Example Konglish Sentence:

The manager was so nice and gave us _service_.

The manager was so nice and gave us a free dessert for a _service_.

Translated to American English:

The manager was so nice and gave us a _complementary_ dessert.

SUPER 슈퍼

Meaning in Konglish:

Usually a small grocery store, smaller than a large supermarket but larger than a corner store or bodega

Example Konglish Sentence:

I went to the _super_ this weekend.

Translated to American English:

I went to the _grocery store_ this weekend.

HOUSE, HOMES, AND LIVING

12

Scan for Audio

AIR CON 에어컨

Meaning in Konglish:

Air conditioner, A/C

Example Konglish Sentence:

It's hot. Can we please use _air con_?

Translated to American English:

It's hot. Can we please use the _air conditioner_ / _A/C_?

APART (APT) 아파트

Meaning in Konglish:

Apartment

Example Konglish Sentence:

My _apart_ is fairly old.

You can come to my _apart_.

Translated to American English:

My _apartment_ is fairly old.

You can come to my _apartment_.

CARPET 카펫

Meaning in Konglish:
A rug

Example Konglish Sentence:
My friends just bought beautiful new _carpet_ for their dining room.

Translated to American English:
My friends just bought a beautiful new _rug_ for their dining room.

CLOSET 클로젯

Meaning in Konglish:
A wardrobe or armoire

Example Konglish Sentence:
I need to buy some new furniture. My wife and I are looking for a new _closet_.

Translated to American English:
I need to buy some new furniture. My wife and I are looking for a new _wardrobe_/_armoire_.

CONSENT 콘센트

Meaning in Konglish:

Electrical outlet

Example Konglish Sentence:

Where is the _consent_?

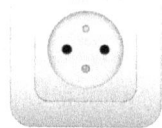

Translated to American English:

Where is the (electrical) _outlet_?

DRESS ROOM 드레스 룸

Meaning in Konglish:

A walk-in closet or hallway closet

Example Konglish Sentence:

I need to clean up my _dress room_.

Translated to American English:

I need to clean up my _closet_.

INTERPHONE 인터폰

Meaning in Konglish:

The intercom box usually at the entrance of an apartment or building that guests use to call up so the resident can buzz them in when they arrive

Example Konglish Sentence:

Call me on the _interphone_ when you arrive.

Translated to American English:

Call me on the _intercom_ when you arrive.

Call me when you arrive, and I'll buzz you up.

MY ROOM 마이룸

Meaning in Konglish:

This could mean any room of a house/building that you are using as yours. It could mean your office, apartment unit, living room, bedroom, etc.

Example Konglish Sentence:

Please come to _my room_ to discuss this issue.

Let's meet at _my room_; then we can go to the restaurant together.

Translated to American English:

Please come to _my office_ to discuss the issue.

Let's meet at _my apartment_; then we can go to the restaurant together.

ONE ROOM 원룸

Meaning in Konglish:

A studio apartment that is rented by the month and is usually furnished

Example Konglish Sentence:

A lot of my friends live in a _one room_.

Translated to American English:

A lot of my friends live in _studio apartments_.

OFFICETEL 오피스텔

Meaning in Konglish:

This is similar to _one room_ but more upscale. It's essentially a furnished studio apartment inside a building that also rents out units as office space. This provides an option for people to live and work in the same building.

Example Konglish Sentence:

I rented a cheap _officetel_.

Translated to American English:

I rented a _cheap studio apartment that I also use as my office_.

OUTSIDE 밖에/외부에서

Meaning in Konglish:

This can mean out of one's house or office or current place (so this could be at a restaurant or the mall or a museum). "Let's go *outside* for dinner," is a suggestion to go out to a restaurant for dinner. "I didn't go *outside* for one week," might mean you went outside in your yard, but you didn't leave your house. It's very similar to how we use *go out* in American English.

Example Konglish Sentence:

We ate _outside_ on Friday.

Translated to American English:

We ate _out_ on Friday.

We ate _at a restaurant_ on Friday.

Rox/Lox 락스

Meaning in Konglish:

Clorox or Bleach

Example Konglish Sentence:

My toilet overflowed, so I had to use _rox_ in the bathroom.

Translated to American English:

My toilet overflowed, so I had to use _bleach_/_Clorox_ in the bathroom.

Korean Life & Culture – Cleaning Bathrooms

One of my students told me she cleans her bathroom with "rox" in the USA since bathrooms don't have a central drain like they usually do in Korea. Of couse, this led to a long and confusing conversation about how one might clean a bathroom with rocks, but once I understood Clorox, things made a lot more sense. While you can find Western-style bathrooms in some houses and apartments, a typical Korean bathroom has some key differences. Most Korean bathrooms have a central drain in the middle of the floor. This allows you to get water anywhere in the bathroom without worrying about clean-up. In some bathrooms, you might not even have a proper bathtub or shower, rather just a handheld shower head, allowing you to stand anywhere you'd like instead of in one confined area since everything will go down that central drain anyway! Many Koreans say this makes cleaning much easier than in a typical American bathroom. Just spray water everywhere; use soap or whichever clearner you'd like; then spray it clean once more to rinse, and it all drains out. Open the window; let it air dry; and you're good to go!

But Where is the Shower Curtain?

My first time in Korea, I was around 20 years old and had no idea there were such different expectations for showering. The first night, my friend pointed me to the bathroom at her aunt's house, where we were staying, and politely told me I could shower first. When I entered, I noticed there was water splashed around everywhere including on the toilet seat, the sink, and the mirror. I didn't think too much of it and just assumed maybe my friend's teenage boy cousin had previously showered messily and dripped water everywhere.

As I started to get into the bathtub, I noticed there was no shower head to stand under, only a handheld one stationed at waist-height. I turned on the water and went to close the shower curtain but realized there wasn't one. I paused, baffled. What should I do?! How am I supposed to shower without a shower curtain?! The water will go EVERYWHERE! It will be a huge rude mess! I turned off the water for a minute and just sat there thinking. I was too embarrassed to ask my friend – I couldn't imagine we had different cultures about how to properly take a shower! In the end, I couldn't figure out what to do, so I squatted down awkwardly in the bathtub and showered the best I could to avoid getting water outside of the basin. When I finally got the courage to bring it up to my friend later, we both laughed in surprise because neither of us had ever expected that taking a shower could involve cultural differences!

So when you visit Korea, as long as you see that trusty central drain in the bathroom, remember you can shower freely without fear of water splashing outside of set areas like a bathtub!

SENIOR TOWN 시니어 타운

Meaning in Konglish:

Retirement home, retirement community, nursing home, assisted living home or community

Example Konglish Sentence:

Her grandmother lives in a _senior town_.

Translated to American English:

Her grandmother lives in a _retirement home_.

SILVER TOWN 실버타운

Meaning in Konglish:

Retirement home, retirement community, nursing home, assisted living home or community

Example Konglish Sentence:

Her grandmother lives in a _silver town_.

Translated to American English:

Her grandmother lives in a _retirement home_.

SHOWER BATH 샤워 목욕

Meaning in Konglish:

A bathtub/shower combination that is found in many American residences

Example Konglish Sentence:

He is in the _shower bath_. Most American houses have _shower baths_.

Translated to American English:

He is in the _shower_.

He is in the _bath(tub)_. Some American houses have _bathtub/shower combos_.

SHOWER BOOTH 샤워 부스

Meaning in Konglish:

A stand-alone shower that doesn't have a bathtub combined with it

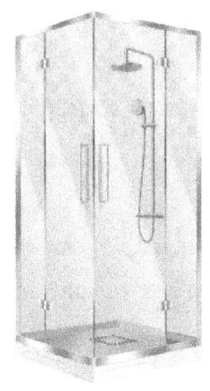

Example Konglish Sentence:

He is in the _shower booth_.

Translated to American English:

He is in the _shower_.

STAND 스탠드

Meaning in Konglish:

A tall floor lamp

Example Konglish Sentence:

The room is dark. We should buy a *stand* to put in the corner.

Translated to American English:

The room is dark. We should buy a *floor lamp* to put in the corner.

VERANDA 베란다

Meaning in Konglish:

Balcony

Example Konglish Sentence:

I have many plants on my *veranda*.

Translated to American English:

I have many plants on my *balcony*.

13

APPLIANCES

Scan for Audio

COOKER 쿡커

Meaning in Konglish:

A cook or a chef

Example Konglish Sentence:

He's a _cooker_ at the new restaurant.

Translated to American English:

He's a _chef_ at the new restaurant.

DRYER 드라이어

Meaning in Konglish:

Hair dryer

Example Konglish Sentence:

I need to use the _dryer_ to make my hair look good.

Translated to American English:

I need to use the _hair dryer_ to make my hair look good.

GAS RANGE 가스렌지

Meaning in Konglish:

Gas stove

Example Konglish Sentence:

Please turn off the _gas range_ before going out.

Translated to American English:

Please turn off the _stove_ before going out.

INDUCTION 인덕션

Meaning in Konglish:

Electric stove or induction cooktop

Example Konglish Sentence:

Please turn off the _induction_ before going out.

Translated to American English:

Please turn off the _stove_ before going out.

MIXER 믹서

Meaning in Konglish:

Blender

Example Konglish Sentence:

Put fruit and vegetables in the _mixer_ to make a smoothie.

Translated to American English:

Put fruit and vegetables in the _blender_ to make a smoothie.

REFRIDGE 냉장고

Meaning in Konglish:

Fridge or refrigerator

Example Konglish Sentence:

The milk is in the _refridge_.

Translated to American English:

The milk is in the _fridge_.
The milk is in the _refrigerator_.

REMO CON / REMOTE CON 리모콘

Meaning in Konglish:

Remote control

Example Konglish Sentence:

Can you pass me the _remo con_?

Translated to American English:

Can you pass me the _remote_?

STAINLESS 스테인리스

Meaning in Konglish:

Stainless steel

Example Konglish Sentence:

I want _stainless_ bowls because they won't break.

Translated to American English:

I want _stainless steel_ bowls because they won't break.

14

SOCIAL LIFE

Scan for Audio

EVENT 이벤트

Meaning in Konglish:

1. A sale or promotional event at a store

2. A special celebration, both big and small

3. A *proposal event* is specifically a grand and extravagant marriage proposal

Example Konglish Sentence:

The store is having an *event*.

My sister is having an *event* tomorrow.

Translated to American English:

The store is having a *sale*.

My sister is having a *birthday party* tomorrow.

A Birthday Event

One of my students living in the United States went to a nice restaurant for her 7-year-old son's birthday. "The restaurant had an event for his birthday," she told me. I thought maybe she meant they had a birthday party there and planned activities and food and fun for a big group of her son's friends. Actually, she meant that they served him a free piece of cake and sang happy birthday like they do at most restaurants. In Konglish, an *event* can mean even something small like this!

FAMILY NAME 패밀리 네임

Meaning in Konglish:

Last name

Example Konglish Sentence:

What's your _family name_?

Translated to American English:

What's your _last name_?

NIGHT 나이트

Meaning in Konglish:

A night club

Example Konglish Sentence:

A lot of young people in Korea go to _night_.

Translated to American English:

A lot of young people in Korea go to _night clubs_.

A lot of young people in Korea go to _clubs_.

A lot of young people in Korea go _clubbing_.

SCHEDULE 스케줄

Meaning in Konglish:

Plans

Example Konglish Sentence:

I can't meet you Monday. I have a *schedule*.

Translated to American English:

I can't meet you Monday. I have *plans*.

Common Conversations

This is a common conversation I have with Korean students:

Me – Do you want to meet me Tuesday at 10am?

Student – I'm sorry. I have a schedule on Tuesday. Can you meet me on Wednesday? I don't have any schedule then.

SILLY 씰리

Meaning in Konglish:

Foolish; only used as an insult or a negative meaning, not playfully as we often use silly in American English

Example Konglish Sentence:

I was too _silly_ that I got a warning from my teacher.

Translated to American English:

I was acting _foolish_, so I got a warning from my teacher.

The Silly Cheater

Years ago, a friend of mine was dating a terrible guy for several years who cheated on her with a woman in Korea and later again with a third woman. When my friend found out the extent of everything and ended things with the guy, she found the Korean woman on social media and discovered that she believed the guy was also _her_ boyfriend. My friend reached out to her on social media to let her know that their man was a liar and a cheater to hopefully save her from some future pain. The Korean woman (understandably) did not believe this at all initially and replied in her message to my friend with, "Hello Silly, [angry words about the situation]..." The message felt confusing. "Hello silly" sounded light, unoffensive, and even playful, but then the message followed with angry insults. My friend and I joked, texting each other, "Hey Silly..." in jest about the situation for months until I finally learned from a Korean student that _silly_ is typically only used as an insult and is more along the lines of calling someone "stupid" or expletives.

SNS 에스엔에스

Meaning in Konglish:

Social media

Example Konglish Sentence:

Let's follow each other on _SNS_.

Translated to American English:

Let's follow each other on _social media_.

UNTACT 언택

Meaning in Konglish:

Contactless

Example Konglish Sentence:

Nowadays, people use a lot of _untact_ machines.

Translated to American English:

Nowadays, people use a lot of _contactless_ machines.

15

RELATIONSHIPS AND DATING

Scan for Audio

BOOKING 부킹

Meaning in Konglish:

At many clubs in Korea, you can request a *booking*. This is basically where the club staff sets up two single girls who came together with two single guys who came together. It's basically a set up or an introduction to potential dates at a club.

Example Konglish Sentence:

I had a *booking* at a club last week.

Translated to American English:

I was *introduced to someone for a date* at a club last week.

I was *set up with someone* at a club last week.

HUNTING 헌팅

Meaning in Konglish:

The act of asking for someone's number in order to ask them out on a date

Example Konglish Sentence:

I *got hunted* by a guy I do not know at the beach.

Translated to American English:

I *got asked out* by a guy I do not know at the beach.

A guy at the beach I didn't know *asked for my number*.

MEETING 미팅

Meaning in Konglish:

This is a blind date, blind double date, or blind group date, usually for more than one couple, usually set up by mutual friends (or possibly an organization)

Example Konglish Sentence:

I met my husband at a _meeting_ through my friends.

Translated to American English:

I met my husband on a _blind date_ that my friends set up.

I met my husband on a _blind double date_ that my friends set up.

MY/OUR COUPLE (OUR BOO BOO) 부부

Meaning in Konglish:

Both people of a romantic couple

Example Konglish Sentence:

Did _your couple_ go to the party?

Translated to American English:

Did _you and your boyfriend_ go to the party?

Did _you and your girlfriend_ go to the party?

Did _you and your wife_ go to the party?

Did _you and your husband_ go to the party?

Did _you and your spouse/partner/significant other_ go to the party?

PROPOSE 프로포즈

Meaning in Konglish:

A marriage proposal that is usually grand and extravagant

Example Konglish Sentence:

He _proposed_ her at a park.

His _propose_ was so amazing.

Translated to American English:

He _proposed_ to her at a park.

His _proposal_ was so amazing.

SKINSHIP 스킨십

Meaning in Konglish:

Physical intimacy, physical contact, holding hands, PDA

Example Konglish Sentence:

My wife loves _skinship_.

Translated to American English:

My wife likes _physical affection_.

SOLO 솔로

Meaning in Konglish:

Single, doesn't have a boyfriend/girlfriend/husband/wife/partner/etc.

Example Konglish Sentence:

He's _solo_, so he's going to the party alone.

Translated to American English:

He's _single_, so he's going to the party alone.

THEIR EYES ARE HIGH 눈이 높다

Meaning in Konglish:

When someone's standards or expectations are too high or unrealistic

Example Konglish Sentence:

Her mom always tells her she will be _solo_ because _her eyes are too high_, but she'd rather be single than settle for someone who doesn't treat her with respect.

Translated to American English:

Her mom always tells her she will be _single_ because her _standards are too high / she's too picky_, but she'd rather be single than settle for someone who doesn't treat her with respect.

WEDDING MARCH 웨딩마치

Meaning in Konglish:

Wedding, bridal entrance, bridal procession, walking down the aisle

Example Konglish Sentence:

300 people came to our _wedding march_.

During her _wedding march_, she tripped on her wedding dress.

Translated to American English:

300 people came to our _wedding_.

While she was _walking down the aisle_, she tripped on her wedding dress.

16

FEELINGS, EMOTIONS, DESCRIBING CHARACTER AND PERSONALITY

Scan for Audio

CENTI 센치

Meaning in Konglish:

1. Centimeter

2. Sad, emotional, moody, sentimental

Example Konglish Sentence:

I'm so _centi_ today.

My little plant is now 10 _centi_.

Translated to American English:

I'm so _emotional_ today.

My little plant is now 10 _centimeters_ tall!

CHEER UP 치얼업

Meaning in Konglish:

Cheer, cheer for

Example Konglish Sentence:

She's going to _cheer up_ the football team.

I _cheered up_ a lot at the game yesterday.

Translated to American English:

She's going to _cheer for_ the football team.

I _cheered_ a lot at the game yesterday.

CHIC 시크

Meaning in Konglish:

This is used with a slightly more negative meaning than in American English. It's used to describe someone who is fashionable and cool-looking but who appears cold and unapproachable on the exterior. Someone *chic* typically doesn't show a lot of emotion and is very attractive, stylish, and intimidating in appearance.

Example Konglish Sentence:

She is very *chic* and cool.

Translated to American English:

She is *fashionable, intimidating, unapproachable*, and cool.

COMPLEX 콤플렉스

Meaning in Konglish:

An insecurity or something that makes a person feel self-conscious

Example Konglish Sentence:

My *complex* is my low nose.

Translated to American English:

I *feel self-conscious about* my nose.

I feel *insecure* about my nose.

FIGHTING 파이팅/화이팅

Meaning in Konglish:

You can do it! Good luck! Way to go! Let's get it! Often said while raising a closed fist in the air for inspiration and oomph, *Fighting!* is a general shout or cheer of encouragement or rally to cheer on your friend or your favorite sports team.

Example Konglish Sentence:

Fighting! You can do it!

Translated to American English:

Go team! You can do it! (cheering for a team)

You got this! You can do it! (encouraging a friend or person)

FROZEN 프로즌

Meaning in Konglish:

Nervous

Example Konglish Sentence:

When the teacher came in, the boy was *frozen*.

I was *frozen* during the test.

Translated to American English:

When the teacher came in, the boy got *nervous*.

I was *nervous* during the test.

MANIA 매니아

Meaning in Konglish:

A big fan of something, connoisseur, really into or obsessed with something. *Mania* typically has a neutral or positive meaning rather than a negative one.

Example Konglish Sentence:

She is Korean drama *mania*. She knows almost all the dramas streaming now.

Translated to American English:

She is a *huge fan* of Korean dramas. / She is *obsessed with* Korean dramas. / She is *really into* Korean dramas. She knows almost all the K dramas streaming now.

MENTAL 멘탈

Meaning in Konglish:

Mentality, attitude; level of motivation, determination, resilience, perseverance, or ability to face a challenge or difficulty

Example Konglish Sentence:

- My computer had a serious problem, but I resolved it by doing X, Y, and Z.
- My *mental* is really weak. I would have just given up and bought a new one.

Translated to American English:

- My computer had a serious problem, but I resolved it by doing X, Y, and Z.
- Honestly, *I'm not that motivated or determined* / *I feel unable to face that challenge*. I would have just given up and bought a new one.

MIND 마인드

Meaning in Konglish:

Put your mind to something, have your mind set on something, want or intend to do something

Example Konglish Sentence:

He _has a mind to_ learn Korean.

Translated to American English:

He _wants to_ learn Korean.

He _has his mind set on_ learning Korean.

He _intends to_ learn Korean.

MIND CONTROL 마인드 컨트롤

Meaning in Konglish:

Calm yourself down, keep composure, soothe your mind, self-management, self-help, self-control, get yourself in the right mindset, pump yourself up

Example Konglish Sentence:

I like to read _mind control_ books.

He had to do _mind control_ before he gave his speech.

Translated to American English:

I like to read _self-help_ / _self-improvement_ books.

He had to _calm his nerves_ / _get in the right mindset_ / _get in the right mental space_ / _get mentally prepared_ / _do some mindfulness and breathing exercises_ before he gave his speech.

MULTI-PLAYER 멀티플레이어

Meaning in Konglish:

A person who can multi-task well

Example Konglish Sentence:

She's a _multi-player_.

Translated to American English:

She's _good at multi-tasking_.

SPORTS AND ACTIVITIES

Scan for Audio

BACK NUMBER 백 넘버

Meaning in Konglish:

Jersey number

Example Konglish Sentence:

What's his _back number_?

It's 13.

Translated to American English:

What's his _jersey number_?

It's 13.

BICYCLE HIKING

Meaning in Konglish:

Mountain biking

Example Konglish Sentence:

We went _bicycle hiking_ on the scenic trail last weekend.

Translated to American English:

We went _mountain biking_ on the scenic trail last weekend.

HANDY 핸디

Meaning in Konglish:

1. Handicap in golf
2. Something easy to carry

Example Konglish Sentence:

He had a golf _handy_ of 7.
The box is _handy_.

Translated to American English:

He had a _handicap_ of 7.
The box is _easy to carry_.

HIKING 하이킹

Meaning in Konglish:

The term *hiking* in Konglish covers a large range of activities and can actually include scenic biking, hiking, overnight hiking, trekking, and backpacking. This can sometimes include climbing as well. Many Koreans say the key feature of *hiking* is that you follow a marked trail or pre-planned route in nature. Typically, *hiking* refers to a longer, often all day or overnight, and more intense activity than just a two or three-hour hike.

Example Konglish Sentence:

We love to go *hiking* with our bicycle to the viewpoint.

In Colombia, you can take a three-day *hike* through the jungle to the ancient ruins of an ancient city called the Lost City.

Translated to American English:

We love to *bike* to the viewpoint.

In Colombia, you can take a three-day *trek* through the jungle to the ruins of an ancient city called The Lost City.

POCKETBALL 포켓볼

Meaning in Konglish:
Pool, billiards

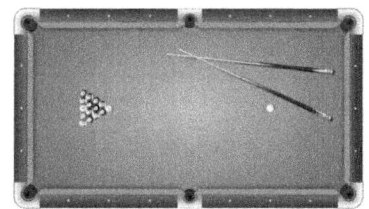

Example Konglish Sentence:
He was the _pocketball_ champion at his school.

Translated to American English:
He was the _pool_ champion at his school.

He was the _billiards_ champion at his school.

RUNNING MACHINE 러닝머신

Meaning in Konglish:
Treadmill

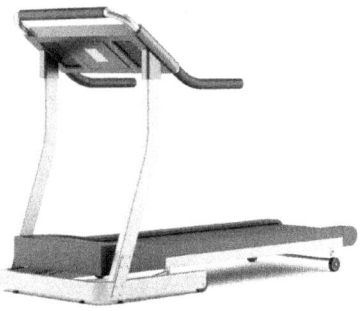

Example Konglish Sentence:
We decided to buy a _running machine_.

Translated to American English:
We decided to buy a _treadmill_.

SKIN SCUBA 스킨스쿠버

Meaning in Konglish:

Scuba diving or a scuba diver

Example Konglish Sentence:

I like to _skin scuba_ in Jeju Island.

Translated to American English:

I like to _scuba dive_ in Jeju Island.

SPORTS DANCING 스포츠 댄싱

Meaning in Konglish:

Competitive ballroom dancing

Example Konglish Sentence:

She has been doing _sports dancing_ for five years.

Translated to American English:

She has been doing _competitive ballroom dancing_ for five years.

SPORTSMAN 스포츠맨/운동선수

Meaning in Konglish:

Professional athlete

Example Konglish Sentence:

He's one of the most famous *sportsmen* in Korea.

Translated to American English:

He's one of the most famous *professional athletes* in Korea.

TREKKING 트레킹

Meaning in Konglish:

Trekking in Konglish is most similar to hiking, backpacking, trekking, or backcountry hiking. *Trekking* can be a simple hike or refer to a difficult or multi-day trip in nature where you do not follow a set trail, path, or route in areas of nature that do not typically have access by usual roads or public transportation.

Example Konglish Sentence:

We *trekked* to the top of Baegundae in the National Park near Seoul. It took us around five hours to go all the way to the peak and back down.

Translated to American English:

We *hiked* to the top of Baegundae in the National Park near Seoul. It took us around five hours to go all the way to the peak and back down.

MUSIC, MOVIES, AND ENTERTAINMENT

BACK DANCER 백 댄서

Meaning in Konglish:

Backup dancer

Example Konglish Sentence:

That singer has good _back dancers_.

Translated to American English:

That singer has good _backup dancers_.

BACK SINGER 백 싱어

Meaning in Konglish:

Backup singer, background singer

Example Konglish Sentence:

The _back singers_ make the music better.

Translated to American English:

The _backup singers_ make the music better.

CHORUS 코러스

Meaning in Konglish:

A choir or backup singers

Example Konglish Sentence:

I heard that _chorus_ before.

Translated to American English:

I've heard that _choir_ before.

CM SONG 씨엠송

Meaning in Konglish:

A jingle or catchy music usually for an advertisement or commercial

Example Konglish Sentence:

That brand is famous for its _CM song_.

Translated to American English:

That brand is famous for its _jingle_.

Docu 다큐/다큐맨어리

Meaning in Konglish:

Documentary

Example Konglish Sentence:

I get mad when I watch a _docu_ about the Korean War.

Translated to American English:

I get mad when I watch _documentaries_ about the Korean War.

Drama 드라마

Meaning in Konglish:

TV show/series, especially Korean dramas. _Drama_ doesn't necessarily mean the genre is drama. It can include most genres of shows that run as a series and aren't sitcoms. Sometimes American TV shows like The Office or Grey's Anatomy are called _American Drama (miguk drama)_ or _mid (**miguk** drama)_ for short.

Example Konglish Sentence:

What kind of _dramas_ do you watch? I enjoy comedies.

Translated to American English:

What kind of _shows_ do you watch? I enjoy comedies.

EPISODE 에피소드

Meaning in Konglish:

A story or something that happened

Example Konglish Sentence:

I have to tell you an *episode* that happened yesterday.

Translated to American English:

I have to tell you a *story* about something that happened yesterday.

I have to tell you *what happened* yesterday.

FAN SIGN(ING) 팬싸인회

Meaning in Konglish:

When a celebrity holds a big event where they give out autographs to fans

Example Konglish Sentence:

I will go to G-Dragon's *fan sign* meeting! He's giving his *sign*!

Translated to American English:

I will go to G-Dragon's *meet and greet*! He's giving out *autographs*!

FANTASTIC 판타스틱

Meaning in Konglish:

Fantasy (genre)

Example Konglish Sentence:

I like _fantastic_ movies.

Translated to American English:

I like _fantasy_ movies.

GAGMAN/GAGWOMAN 개그맨/개그우먼

Meaning in Konglish:

A comedian, often one who does physical/slapstick comedy, sketch comedy, or general entertainment rather than just traditional stand-up

Example Konglish Sentence:

Son, if you become a _gagman_, I will accept your decision, but you won't make _big money_.

Translated to American English:

Son, if you become a _comedian_, I will accept your decision, but you won't make _very much money_.

HIGHTEEN STAR 하이틴스타

Meaning in Konglish:

A famous celebrity movie star or musician who is a teenager

Example Konglish Sentence:

The *highteen star* sings well too!

Translated to American English:

The *teenage celebrity* sings well too!

MELODRAMA 멜로드라마

Meaning in Konglish:

Usually a love story with a sad ending, a romantic drama

Example Konglish Sentence:

She really likes to watch *melodramas*.

Translated to American English:

She really likes to watch *romantic dramas*.

PIERROT 피에로

Meaning in Konglish:

Clown

Example Konglish Sentence:

I worked part-time wearing a _pierrot_
costume.

Translated to American English:

I worked part-time wearing a _clown_ costume.

"English" that isn't English at All

There are several Konglish terms that did not actually come from English at all! As I'm sure you can tell, this is one of them. I'll never forget the time a student told me there was a "Pierrot at the restaurant on Saturday." Thinking she was pronouncing something wrong, I asked her to repeat the word a couple of times. Still confused, I told her I wasn't familiar with a "Pierrot", but she insisted it was an English word that everyone knew. I asked her to spell it for me. P-I-E-R-R-O-T, she wrote out on the piece of paper on the table. I wasn't familiar with Konglish at the time, and I told her I had never seen this word before in my life. In that moment, I think she was torn between whether to accept that her American teacher didn't know common English words or whether a word she had believed for years was English, in fact wasn't English at all. In the end, she searched for a picture, and we found that this word came from the famous French pantomime character with the same name.

SIGN 싸인

Meaning in Konglish:

Your signature or written name or an autograph from a celebrity

Example Konglish Sentence:

Can I have your _sign_ here?

Translated to American English:

Can I have your _signature_ here?

TALENT 탤런트

Meaning in Konglish:

A person who is famous for acting in K-dramas. It doesn't apply to Broadway show actors/actresses or musicians.

Example Konglish Sentence:

My favorite _talent_ is filming a new drama.

Translated to American English:

My favorite _K-drama actor_ is filming a new K-drama.

TELEBI 텔레비

Meaning in Konglish:

TV

Example Konglish Sentence:

My hobby is watching _telebi_.

Translated to American English:

My hobby is watching _TV_.

TOP STAR 탑스타

Meaning in Konglish:

An A-list celebrity or extremely famous movie star

Example Konglish Sentence:

She is a _top star_ in Korea.

Translated to American English:

She is an _A-list celebrity_ in Korea.

She is a _huge movie star_ in Korea.

TV SHOW TV 쇼

Meaning in Konglish:

Talk show or late-night talk show on TV

Example Konglish Sentence:

- What _TV shows_ do you like?
- Oh, I don't watch _TV shows_. I only like dramas like This is Us and Grey's Anatomy.

Translated to American English:

- What _talk shows_ do you like?
- Oh, I don't watch _talk shows_. I only like (TV) shows like This is Us and Grey's Anatomy.

19

TRAVEL

Scan for Audio

CARRIER 케리어

Meaning in Konglish:

Suitcase or carry-on suitcase

Example Konglish Sentence:

Are you bringing a _carrier_ with you on the plane?

How many _carriers_ are you bringing on the trip?

Translated to American English:

Are you bringing a _carry-on suitcase_ with you on the plane?

How many _suitcases_ are you bringing on the trip?

GOODS 굿즈

Meaning in Konglish:

Souvenirs

Example Konglish Sentence:

We need to get some _goods_ on our vacation to bring back to our friends.

Translated to American English:

We need to get some _souvenirs_ on our vacation to bring back to our friends.

HAND(Y) CARRY 핸드 케리

Meaning in Konglish:

Carry-on bag

Example Konglish Sentence:

Do you have a *handy carry*?

Do you have a *hand carry*?

Translated to American English:

Do you have a *carry-on bag*?

HOCANCE 호캉스

Meaning in Konglish:

A staycation where the focus of the vacation is the hotel rather than a beach or other destination to sightsee. People usually choose a nice hotel or resort for this type of vacation, and many Korean hotels advertise special *hocance* packages.

Example Konglish Sentence:

I really want to have a *hocance*.

Do you know any hotels that are good for a *hocance*?

Translated to American English:

I really want to have a *staycation* at a hotel.

Do you know any *hotels* that are good for this?

MORNING CALL 모닝 콜

Meaning in Konglish:

Wake-up call at a hotel

Example Konglish Sentence:

Can I get a *morning call* at 7 a.m.?

Translated to American English:

Can I get a *wake-up call* at 7 a.m.?

OUTING 아우팅

Meaning in Konglish:

A picnic

Example Konglish Sentence:

We had an *outing* at the park this weekend.

Translated to American English:

We had a *picnic* at the park this weekend.

ROUNDING 라운딩

Meaning in Konglish:

1. A tour
2. Playing a round of golf

Example Konglish Sentence:

Guests from Korea will visit our hospital. We will give them a hospital _rounding_.

Do you want to go for a _rounding_ tomorrow?

Translated to American English:

Guests from Korea will visit our hospital. We will give them a hospital _tour_.

Do you want to _play (a round of) golf_ tomorrow?

TOP, TAP 탑

Meaning in Konglish:

Tower

Example Konglish Sentence:

We didn't go to the top of the Eiffel _top_.

Translated to American English:

We didn't go to the top of the Eiffel _Tower_.

The Top of the Top

I once had this confusing conversation with a student.

Me – How was your trip to France?!

Student – Great! We visited so many places, but we didn't go to the top.

Me – The top of what?

Student – We didn't go to the top in Paris.

Me – ...? But the top of what?

(Student searches for a picture of the Eiffel Tower and shows me)

Me – Ohhh, you didn't go to the top of the Eiffel Tower. Did you go to the bottom and take some pictures around it?

Student – No, we didn't go to the Eiffel. That's what I'm saying.

20

CARS AND TRANSPORTATION

Scan for Audio

ACCEL 악셀/액셀

Meaning in Konglish:

Accelerator, gas pedal

Example Konglish Sentence:

There is a problem with my car. When I
press the _accel_, my car doesn't move.

Translated to American English:

There is a problem with my car.
When I step on the _accelerator_ / _gas pedal_ my car doesn't move.

AUTOBI 오토바이

Meaning in Konglish:

Motorcycle

Example Konglish Sentence:

It's fun to ride an _autobi_.

Translated to American English:

It's fun to ride a _motorcycle_.

BACK MIRROR 백미러

Meaning in Konglish:

Rearview mirror

Example Konglish Sentence:

I saw my kids fighting in the _back mirror_.

Translated to American English:

I saw my kids fighting in the _rearview mirror_.

CARAVAN 카라반

Meaning in Konglish:

Camper or camping trailer or travel
trailer

Example Konglish Sentence:

Let's go camping in a _caravan_!

Translated to American English:

Let's go camping with a _camping trailer_!

CAMPING CAR 캠핑카

Meaning in Konglish:

RV, Camper, Camping trailer, Travel trailer

Example Konglish Sentence:

Let's go camping in a _camping car_!

Translated to American English:

Let's go camping with an _RV_/_camper_!

CAR CENTER 카센터

Meaning in Konglish:

Auto shop, auto repair shop

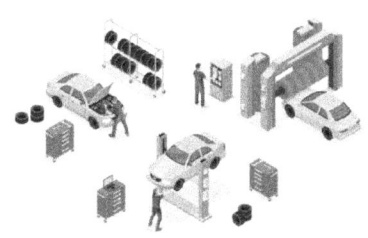

Example Konglish Sentence:

I'm going to the _car center_ to fix my car today.

Translated to American English:

I'm going to the _auto repair shop_ to fix my car today.

CLAXON 클락션

Meaning in Konglish:

Car horn

Example Konglish Sentence:

I hate driving here because people always use the _Claxon_.

Translated to American English:

I hate driving here because people always honk the _horn_.

HANDLE 핸들

Meaning in Konglish:

Car steering wheel

Example Konglish Sentence:

I took my car to the *car center* because my *handle* has a problem.

Translated to American English:

I took my car to the *auto shop* because my *steering wheel* has a problem.

KICKBOARD 킥보드

Meaning in Konglish:

A non-motorized scooter

Example Konglish Sentence:

My niece and nephew love to ride their *kickboards* to the neighborhood park.

Translated to American English:

My niece and nephew love to ride their *scooters* to the neighborhood park.

MISSION 미션

Meaning in Konglish:

Transmission

Example Konglish Sentence:

My *car mission* is broken; I'm afraid it's going to be expensive to fix.

Translated to American English:

My *car transmission* is broken; I'm afraid it's going to be expensive to fix.

OPEN CAR 오픈 카

Meaning in Konglish:

Convertible

Example Konglish Sentence:

I want to buy an *open car*.

Translated to American English:

I want to buy a *convertible*.

PUNK 펑크

Meaning in Konglish:

Flat tire

Example Konglish Sentence:

She had a _punk_ this morning, so she'll be late to the meeting today.

Translated to American English:

She had a _flat tire_ this morning, so she'll be late to the meeting today.

RADIATOR 라디에이터

Meaning in Konglish:

Space heater, portable heater, electric heater

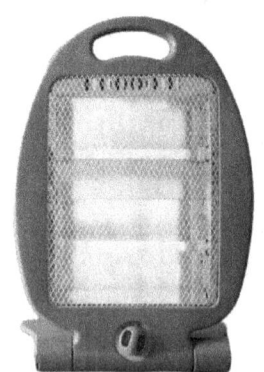

Example Konglish Sentence:

American office buildings are so cold because of the _air con_, but you can buy a _radiator_ at the Korean store.

Translated to American English:

American office buildings are so cold because of the _air conditioner_, but you can buy a _space heater_ at the Korean store.

SCOOTER 스쿠터

Meaning in Konglish:

A moped or similar small motorbike

Example Konglish Sentence:

Riding a _scooter_ is fun.

Translated to American English:

Riding a _moped_ is fun.

SIDE BRAKE 사이드브레이크

Meaning in Konglish:

Parking brake, emergency brake

Example Konglish Sentence:

When I park my car, I always set up my _side brake_.

Translated to American English:

When I park my car, I always use the _parking brake_ / _emergency brake_.

STICKER 벌금딱지

Meaning in Konglish:

A speeding ticket or any ticket from the police

Example Konglish Sentence:

I'm upset because I got a _sticker_.

Translated to American English:

I'm upset because I got a _speeding ticket_.

WINDOW BRUSH / WIPER
윈도우 브러시 / 와이퍼

Meaning in Konglish:

Windshield wipers

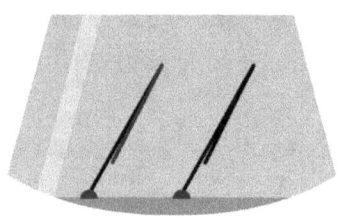

Example Konglish Sentence:

It could be dangerous if your _window brush_ is too old. / It could be dangerous if your _wiper_ is too old.

Translated to American English:

It could be dangerous if your _windshield wipers_ are too old.

TOOLS AND OTHER
USEFUL ITEMS

Scan for Audio

DRIVER 드라이버/도라이바

Meaning in Konglish:

Screwdriver

Example Konglish Sentence:

He bought a _driver_ at L's Hardware.

Translated to American English:

He bought a _screwdriver_ at L's Hardware.

Where Can I Buy a Driver?

I once had this confusing conversation with a student.

Student – My son needs a driver. Do you know where he can buy one?

Me – What do you mean? He needs a taxi?

Student – No.

Me – He needs to rent a car?

Student – No, the car is fine. He doesn't need a ride anywhere.

Me – But you said he needed a driver. What does he need? A golf club?

She then acted out the motion of using a screwdriver and explained that he needed to fix something.

"Ohhhhhhh," I said, "A screwdriver!"

MACGYVER KNIFE 맥가이버 나이프

Meaning in Konglish:

Pocketknife, Swiss Army knife

Example Konglish Sentence:

You can't bring a _MacGyver knife_ on an airplane. They might confiscate it.

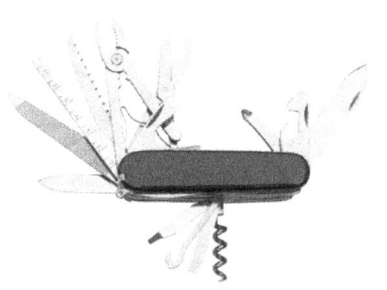

Translated to American English:

You can't bring a _pocketknife_ on an airplane. They might confiscate it.

PINCHER 삘찌

Meaning in Konglish:

Pliers

Example Konglish Sentence:

I need a hammer and some _pinchers_.

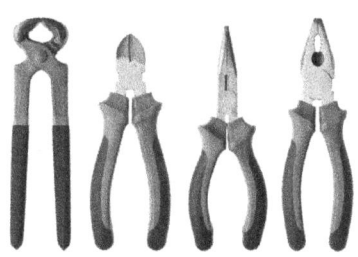

Translated to American English:

I need a hammer and some _pliers_.

POKLAIN 포크레인

Meaning in Konglish:

Excavator

Example Konglish Sentence:

There were many *poklains* building
a big mall in the construction area.

Translated to American English:

There were many *excavators* building
a big mall in the construction area.

TUPPA 타파

Meaning in Konglish:

Tupperware

Example Konglish Sentence:

Are the *tuppa* water bottles BPA-free?

Translated to American English:

Are the *Tupperware* water bottles
BPA-free?

VINYL 비닐

Meaning in Konglish:

Plastic bag

Example Konglish Sentence:

In Korea, you won't find any _vinyl_ bags at major grocery stores.

Translated to American English:

In Korea, you won't find any _plastic_ bags at major grocery stores.

WRAP 랩

Meaning in Konglish:

Plastic wrap, Saran wrap, cling wrap

Example Konglish Sentence:

This _wrap_ is great quality.

Translated to American English:

This _plastic wrap_ is great quality.

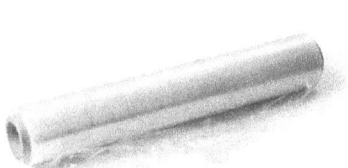

ZIPPER BAG 지퍼 백

Meaning in Konglish:

A ziplock bag or sandwich bag

Example Konglish Sentence:

I put some fruit in the _zipper bag_.

Translated to American English:

I put some fruit in the _ziplock bag_.

22

MISCELLANEOUS

Scan for Audio

Dry 드라이

Meaning in Konglish:

Dry cleaning

Example Konglish Sentence:

I need to _dry_ these clothes.

I need to take these clothes to _dry_.

Translated to American English:

I need to _dry clean_ these clothes.

I need to take these clothes to _dry clean_.

DRY CLEANING
SERVICES

Journal 일지

Meaning in Konglish:

Newspaper or magazine

Example Konglish Sentence:

My friend loves fashion _journals_.

Translated to American English:

My friend loves fashion _magazines_.

ONE SHOT, ONE KILL 원샷 원킬

Meaning in Konglish:

Zero tolerance; one strike and you're out

Example Konglish Sentence:

The company policy on drinking alcohol on the job is _one shot, one kill_.

Translated to American English:

The company policy on drinking alcohol on the job is _zero tolerance_.

The company policy on drinking alcohol on the job is _one strike and you're out_.

OVER 오버

Meaning in Konglish:

Over the top, exaggerated/exaggerating, to over-do something

Example Konglish Sentence:

She is always _over_.

The party was extremely _over_.

Translated to American English:

She is always _over-exaggerating_. / She always _over-exaggerates_.

The party was extremely _over the top_.

The party was _so much better than what I expected_!

Pick Me Up 픽미업

Meaning in Konglish:

Choose me, pick me

Example Konglish Sentence:

Oh, I hope he *picks me up* as the winner.

Translated to American English:

Oh, I hope he *picks me* as the winner.

Paint Colors and A Winner's Ride

A student once told me that she and her husband were planning to paint a room. She said she wanted to "pick up" blue paint, but her husband wanted to "pick up" white paint. I was confused and asked to clarify, "Do you mean you are going to buy the blue paint, and your husband is going to buy the white paint?" No. "Do you mean you are going to paint all the blue parts, and he is going to paint all the white parts?" No. She meant that they couldn't paint yet because they hadn't agreed on which color to use. She wanted to paint the room blue, and her husband wanted to paint the room white; they had to choose which color to use before they could paint.

Another student once explained that he had entered a competition and was hoping they would "pick him up at the end." At first, I thought maybe they were going to arrive at his house, pick him up, and then take him somewhere special to celebrate. He simply meant that he hoped he would be chosen as the winner.

PARADIGM 패러다임

Meaning in Konglish:

Literal or physical example or model

Example Konglish Sentence:

Here is a digital _paradigm_ of the new science complex that will be finished next year.

Translated to American English:

Here is a digital _model_ of the new science complex that will be finished next year.

REVIVE 리바이브

Meaning in Konglish:

Repeat

Example Konglish Sentence:

I'm sorry, I didn't hear that. Can you _revive_, please?

Translated to American English:

I'm sorry, I didn't hear that. Can you _repeat_ it, please?

SHADOW 샤도우

Meaning in Konglish:

Shade

Example Konglish Sentence:

There is some _shadow_ under that tree where we can have our outing.

Translated to American English:

There is some _shade_ under that tree where we can have our picnic.

SPEAK OUT 스픽 아웃

Meaning in Konglish:

Speak louder, speak up

Example Konglish Sentence:

Speak out, Susie, we can't hear you.

Translated to American English:

Speak up, Susie, we can't hear you.

UNISEX 유니섹스

Meaning in Konglish:

Co-ed, unisex, gender-neutral

Example Konglish Sentence:

She plays soccer on a _unisex_ team.

Most students in the U.S. go to _unisex_ schools.

Translated to American English:

She plays soccer on a _co-ed_ team.

Most students in the U.S. go to _co-ed_ schools.

ACKNOWLEDGMENTS

To Yire, first and foremost, thank you for all your hard work and the hours you put into discussing, consulting, and translating in order to help make this book and its counterpart a reality. Thank you for being my first Korean friend. Thank you for teaching me to read and write Hangul, the Korean alphabet, for introducing me to Korean food and culture, and for taking me to beautiful Korea with your family so many years ago. Thank you for showing me life there and patiently translating everything back and forth until you probably didn't want to talk anymore at all. I'm honored to still call you a close friend after 20+ years! There aren't enough words to express my gratitude to have had your help with this book.

To Jaeeun, thank you for believing in this idea with contagious excitement even from the very beginning before it became anything close to a book. I'll never forget those roommate times laughing, telling stories, and sharing our cultures and languages in that old crappy apartment, especially that one summer we camped out under the living room fan when our air conditioner went out in the middle of a hot Houston summer. This book would not have happened if it weren't for those days, all the laughs, the friendship, and the stories we shared. Thank you for all the brainstorming sessions years later, even from half a world away!

To my husband, Kurt, thank you for supporting me throughout this process, for believing in me and reminding me to trust my gut when I doubted myself. Thank for your extensive help in developing the audio resources for this book, for humoring me the many times I leaned over and asked, "Hey, what does this word mean to you?" and for looking through unending piles of variations of layouts, fonts, and photos to give me your thoughtful opinions.

To all my Korean students, past and present, thank you for letting me enter your world, sometimes even your homes and offices; for sharing fresh brewed tea and espresso and cookies like couque d'asse 쿠크다스; for sharing your culture with me as you learned mine, explaining everything from Korean birthing traditions and methods of making kimchi to modern politics and business norms; and for being brave enough and humble enough to continue the ambitious journey of learning and perfecting a new language as adults. Never let yourself feel ashamed of your English mistakes - they are essential for learning!

To all my Korean and Korean American high school students at the hagwon-style tutoring center from 2010-2012, who have since grown up, thank you for all your hard work, your great senses of humor and the laughs during our lessons, and your sharing all the delicious Korean snacks like *hyeonmi-nokcha* 현미녹차, corn hair tea 옥수수수염차, Korean chestnuts, rice cakes, and more. Even more so, thank you for trusting me with vulnerable pieces of your lives as you learned to turn lived experiences into well-written essays. You are inspirations as incredible humans who have walked the often-challenging road straddling two cultures, sometimes each with different expectations of you. As you grow in the life, always remember that who you are is always enough. Your experiences, your opinions, and your stories matter.

To my brother, Daniel, thank you for your valuable help as audio engineer, for taking the time and effort to clean up all the recorded audio for the audio resources to make it all sound pristine. Thank you also for your and Larissa's valuable input along the way regarding style and design.

To everyone else who believed this book was possible and gave encouragement along the way, thank you. Your kind words and support made this book possible.

IMAGE CREDITS

The authors and publishers acknowledge the following sources of copyright material and are grateful for the permissions granted. While every effort has been made, it has not always been possible to identify the sources of all the material used, or to trace all copyright holders. If any omissions are brought to our notice, we will be happy to include the appropriate acknowledgments on reprinting and in the next update, as applicable.

Photographs, Images, & Graphics

The following images are from **Adobe Stock Photos**:

Cover (flags): Aroastock; p. 13 (apps): Scanrail; p. 24 (coffee): olllikeballoon; p. 26 (beer): Scanrail; p. 26 (chicken): Juraiwan; p. 29 (pizza): Alexeg84; p. 31 (corn dog): Lana; p. 32 (worms): Pioneer111; p. 32 (bears): Maren Winter; p. 36 (ice cream): Grigoriy Lukyanov; p. 36 (oreo): Xamtiw; p. 36 (sandwich): Natalie; p. 37 (chicken): Koarakko; p. 38 (drink): Hamara; p. 39 (yogurt): HstrongART; p. 42 (trench coat): Tarzhanova; p. 43 (man): Joycolor; p. 43 (couple): Nathan Hutchcraft; p. 45 (dress): Kathleen; p. 45 (pants): Reshoot; p. 46 (robe): Vectorikart; p. 46 (doctor): ONYXprj; p. 47 (coat): Eric Hood; p. 47 (zipper): Maxim_Kazmin; p. 48 (letterjacket): Nattanopdesign; p. 49 (scarf): Oleh11; p. 50 (dress): Hein Nouwens; p. 52 (jacket): Aleks Kend; p. 52 (hose): Fotoduets; p. 53 (turtleneck): Vitaly Tiagunov; p. 57 (slippers): Bergamont; p. 58 (tracksuit): Nattanopdesign; p. 59 (ladies): Creative Juice; p. 60 (boots): Vadym; p. 60 (shirt): Runrun2; p. 62 (headband): Hanna Syvak; p. 62 (flower): Matoommi; p. 62 (sweatband): Domnitsky; p. 63 (clip): Pixarno; p. 65 (bow): Larisabozhikova; p. 265(fannypack): Godesignz; p. 68 (makeup): SharlottaU; p. 69 (gift): Di Studio; p. 69 (mask): Ирина Коннова; p. 69 (bag): John Kasawa; p. 70 (conditioner): Castecodesign; p. 70 (lipstick): Lumos sp; p. 74 (bodies): Natbasil; p. 82 (Band-Aid): Wabeno; p. 84 (disk): Vonuk; p. 86 (gym): Adrian Hillman; p. 86 (mouthwash): Absent84; p. 87 (cast): Liliia; p. 88 (gym): Adrian Hillman; p. 91 (pain): Papcut design; p. 92 (iv): Stockedup; p. 101 (planner): Andrey Popov; p. 104 (marker): Aliaksandr Ivanou; p. 105 (business cards): Business Card; p. 105 (pens): Dmitri Stalnuhhin; p. 106 (notebook): Nata777_7; p. 112 (pencil) Olga Kovalenko; p. 112 (test): JYPIX; p. 118 (computer): Denis Rozhnovsky; p. 119 (flashlight): Pol Maria; p. 122 (gps): Savanno; p. 122 (computer): Denis Rozhnovsky; p. 123 (selfies): Andreas; p. 126 (money): Kv_san; p. 130 (sale): Atakan; p. 141 (rug): Mguido; p. 141 (wardrobe): Dimamoroz; p. 142 (plug): Oxinoxi; p. 145 (silhouette):

Adrian Hillman; p. 149 (bath): Iryna Petrenko; p. 150 (lamps): New Africa; p. 152 (dryer): Maksim; p. 153 (stoves): YummyBuum; p. 154 (blender): Nito; p. 166 (hands): Tiagozr; p. 175 (lady): REDPIXEL; p. 178 (jersey): FA DESINZ; p. 179 (biking): Anna; p. 181 (pool): Ojovago; p. 181 (treadmill): Tiler84; p. 192 (clown): Alexander Raths; p. 193 (signature): Prezent; p. 198 (suitcase): Coprid; p. 199 (suitcase): Coprid; p. 200 (picnic): M. Studio; p. 202 (tower): HP_Photo; p. 204 (pedal): Ceyhun; p. 204 (motorcycle): Artproba; p. 205 (mirror): Tabthipwatthana; p. 205 (RVs): Studioworkstock; p. 207 (cars): Sensvector; p. 207 (horn): Sirikornt; p. 208 (wheel): Photobeps; p. 208 (scooter): pioneer111; p. 210 (heater): Rjuniormb; p. 211 (moped): Maksym Yemelyanov; p. 212 (windshield): Dumitru; p. 214 (screwdrivers): Spyrakot; p. 215 (knife): Krasyuk; p. 215 (pliers): Donatas1205; p. 216 (digger): Yordan Rusev; p. 216 (Tupperware): SlayStorm; p. 217 (bag): Celeste; p. 217 (wrap): AlenKadr; p. 218 (bag): John Kasawa

The following image is from **Pexels**:

p. 33 (popsicle): Anton Uniqueton

The following images are from **Pixabay**:

p. 15 (discount): MarkRosemaker; p. 16 (ambulance): AzamKamolov; p. 17 (aliens): Alexey_Hulsov; p. 28 (bars): WikimediaImages; p. 38 (dressing): OpenClipart-Vectors; p. 56 (suit): Rintofr; p. 97 (pen): Clker-Free-Vector-Images; p. 106 (laptop): Clker-Free-Vector-Images; p. 118 (camera): Clker-Free-Vector-Images; p. 120 (phone): EsaRiutta; p. 131 (eggs): Dgazdik; p. 182 (dance): 6563351; p. 194 (tv): Jazella

The following images are from **Shutterstock**:

p. 33 (beer): Pushkarevskyy; p. 48 (jacket): Just Dzine; p. 51 (underwear): VikiVector; p. 51 (panties): IVector; p. 63 (clips): ONYXprj; p. 64 (nailpolish): Vector Tradition; p. 90 (vomit): Blueastro; p. 98 (glue): Anton Starikov; p. 99 (clips): Udaix; p. 102 (stapler): Udaix; p. 149 (shower): Sudowoodo; p. 154 (fridge): ApoGapo; p. 182 (diver): Macrovector; p. 187 (choir): Tezzstock; p. 209 (transmission): Gopixa; p. 209 (convertible): Dimitris Leonidas; p. 210 (tire): KsanderDN; p. 220 (dryclean): Kilroy79

Other Images Credits:
p. 233 (author photo): Nate Messarra Photography
p. 233 (logo): design by Renee Blodgett

BIBLIOGRAPHY

Ahn, Soojin. "Perceptions of Konglish by English Language users: An analysis of a reaction video and its comments on YouTube*." *Linguistic Research (KHU ISLI)*, vol. 40, 2023, pp. 151–169, https://doi.org/10.17250/khisli.40..202309.006.

Charles, Quanisha. "Native Korean speakers' attitudes toward *Konglish* as a standardized variety of English." *International Journal of Literature and Arts*, vol. 3, no. 6, 2015, p. 136, https://doi.org/10.11648/j.ijla.20150306.12.

General, Ryan. "Why South Koreans Say 'Hwaiting!'" *NextShark*, 20 Dec. 2021, nextshark.com/south-koreans-say-hwaiting.

Hagens, Sheilagh A. "Attitudes toward Konglish of South Korean Teachers of English in the Province of Jeollanamdo." *Brock University*, 2009.

Jeong, Chan Hee. "The Roles Konglish Plays in the Korean American Community." *Bryn Mawr College*, 2021.

Kim, Hwan-bae. "하이킹 vs. 트레킹, 무엇이 다를까?" 데일리스포츠한국, 2 Aug. 2017, www.dailysportshankook.co.kr/news/articleView.html?idxno=187227.

Lee, Hyon-soo. "Follies of Konglish." *Koreatimes*, 10 June 2014, www.koreatimes.co.kr/www/news/opinon/2016/06/162_158502.html.

McPhail, Sean A. "South Korea's linguistic tangle: English vs. Korean vs. Konglish." *English Today*, vol. 34, no. 1, 7 Aug. 2017, pp. 45–51, https://doi.org/10.1017/s0266078417000244.

Ow, Victoria. "41 Konglish Words You Need to Know to Level up Your Korean Skills." *TheSmartLocal South Korea - Travel, Lifestyle, Culture & Language Guide*, 1 June 2022, thesmartlocal.kr/konglish-words/.

Song, Pyeong-in. "The Evolution of English." 동아일보, www.donga.com/en/article/all/20121226/405367/1.

"South Korea's Hiking Culture Reflects Its Social Pressures." *The Economist*, The Economist Newspaper, www.economist.com/christmas-specials/2020/12/16/south-koreas-hiking-culture-reflects-its-social-pressures.

Tse, Jennifer. "Evolution of Konglish based on the current prevalence and South Korean public attitude towards Konglish." *The George Washington University Undergraduate Review*, vol. 3, 2020, https://doi.org/10.4079/2578-9201.3(2020).10.

INDEX

A/S, 12

Academic class, 96

Academy, 97

Accel, 204

After service, 12

Air con, 140

Americano, 24

Apart (APT), 140

Appl(e), 13

Autobi, 204

Back dancer, 186

Back mirror, 205

Back number, 178

Back singer, 186

Balanced meal, 82

Ball pen, 97

Band, 82

Bar, 25

Bargain, 130

BBQ, 25

BGM, 13

Bicycle hiking, 179

Big money, 126

Big size, 42

BJ, 14

Blue worker, 98

Bodyline, 74

Bond, 98

Booking, 164

Burberry, 42

Camping car, 206

Can maekju, 26

Car center, 207

Caravan, 205

Carpet, 141

Carrier, 198

Centi, 170

CF, 15

Check up, 84

Cheer up, 170

Chic, 171

Chicken, 26

Choco, 28

Chorus, 187

Cider, 27

Circle, 99

Claxon, 207

Clip, 99

Closet, 141

CM Song, 187

Cola, 28

Combi-style, 43

Combi, 29

Combo set, 29

Complex, 171

Computer, 118

Condition, 83

Consent, 142

Cooker, 152

Corner, 130

Couple look, 43

Course, 100

Cream pasta, 30

Cross bag, 62

Cunning, 100

Cushion, 68

D/C, 17

Depart, 131

Department, 131

Diary, 101

Diet, 84

Dika, 118

Disk, 85

Docu, 188

Double eyelid, 75

Doz, 131

Drama, 188

Dress, 45

Dress room, 142

Driver, 214

Dry, 220

Dryer, 152

EMS, 16

Engineer, 101

Episode, 189

Event, 158

Eye remover, 68

Eye shopping, 132

Family name, 159

Fan sign(ing), 189

Fantastic, 190

Fighting, 172

Fitness, 86

Flash, 119

Free size, 44

Frozen, 172

Fund, 126

Gagman, 190

Gagwoman, 190

Game room, 119

Gargle, 86

Gas range, 153

Glamour, 76

Gmap, 120

Golden pants, 45

Goods, 198

Gown, 46

Grocery, 132

Gyps, 87

Hair band, 62

Hair pin, 63

Half coat, 47

Hand carry, 199

Hand phone, 120

Handle, 208

Handmade, 133

Handy, 179

Handy carry, 199

Hard board, 102

Healing time, 87

Health, 88

Healthy meal, 88

Highteen star, 191

Hiking, 180

Hip, 76

Hocance, 199

Homepi, 121

Hop, 30

Hospital, 89

Hot dog, 31

Hotchkiss, 102

Hunting, 164

Ice bar, 33

ID, 121

Image, 78

Induction, 153

Interphone, 143

Jacku, 47

Jelly, 32

Journal, 220

Jumper, 48

Junior, 103

Kickboard, 208

Kk, 16

L size, 54

Lettering, 104

Live beer, 33

LL size, 55

LLL size, 55

Lose my weight, 77

Lunchbox, 34

M size, 54

MacGyver Knife, 215

Magic, 104

Maker, 133

Mania, 173

Manicure, 64

Mart, 134

Meeting, 165

Melodrama, 191

Member ID, 121

Mental, 173

Menu, 34

Mind, 174

Mind control, 174

Mission, 209

Mixer, 154

Morning call, 200

MR, 90

Muffler, 49

Multi-player, 175

My room, 143

My/our couple, 165

Name card, 105

Name pen, 105

Navi, 122

Navigation, 216

Night, 159

Note, 106

Notebook, 106

Officer, 107

Officetel, 144

One by one, 108

One piece, 50

One plus one, 134

One room, 144

One shot, 35

One shot one kill, 221

Open car, 209

OST, 17

Outing, 200

Outlook, 78

Outside, 145

Over, 221

Overeat, 90

Pack, 69

Padding, 52

Panty, 51

Panty stocking, 52

Paradigm, 223

Part, 135

Pass, 91

Pay doctor, 91

PC, 122

Pick me up, 222

Pierrot, 110

Pincher, 215

Pocket money, 127

Pocketball, 181

Poklain, 216

Polar T, 53

Poor, 127

PPT, 19

Print, 108

Propose, 166

PT, 18

Pudding, 35

Punk, 210

Radiator, 210

Read loud, 109

Refridge, 154

Remo con, 155

Rental fee, 128

Revive, 223

Ribbon, 65

Ringer, 92

Rinse, 70

Rouge, 70

Rounding, 201

Rox, 146

Running machine, 181

S size, 53

S-line, 79

Sack, 65

Salary man, 109

Sand, 36

Sauce, 38

Sauce chicken, 37

Schedule, 160

School jumper, 48

Scooter, 211

Secret number, 123

Selca, 123

Self, 136

Self-cam, 124

Senior, 110

Senior town, 148

Separate codi, 56

Service, 136

SF, 17

Shadow, 224

Sharp, 112

Shower bath, 149

Shower booth, 149

Side brake, 211

Sign, 193

Sign pen, 112

Silly, 161

Silver town, 148

Single style suit, 56

Skin, 71

Skin scuba, 182

Skinship, 166

Slippers, 57

Small money, 128

SNS, 162

Solo, 167

Speak out, 224

Specs, 113

Sports dancing, 182

Sportsman, 183

Stainless, 155

Stand, 150

Sticker, 212

Suncream, 92

Super, 137

Talent, 193

Telebi, 194

Their eyes are high, 167

Top Star, 194

Top, 202

Training (bok), 58

Training, 113

Trekking, 183

TT, 20

Tuppa, 216

TV show, 195

Two piece, 59

Unisex, 225

Untact, 162

V-line, 79

Veranda, 150

Vinyl, 217

Visual, 80

Walker, 60

Wedding march, 168

Well being, 93

White, 114

White worker, 114

Window brush, 212

Wiper, 150

Working level people, 115

Wrap, 217

Y shirts, 60

Yogurt, 38

Yoplait, 39

Zero cola, 39

Zipper bag, 218

ABOUT THE AUTHOR

Lauren is the owner and founder of Lauren's Language Lessons, LLC and has been teaching English for over 15 years. She has a degree in International Studies from Texas A&M University and certifications in TEFL/TESL/TESOL for teaching English as a Second Language. Lauren has collaborated with multiple Korean companies to improve employees' English and has taught numerous Korean students of various ages, levels, and professions including business, medicine, education, music, oil & gas, law, technology, research, and more. Lauren is passionate about language and culture and travels every chance she gets. She lives in Houston, Texas with her husband, cat, and dog and enjoys playing soccer and spending time with friends and family.

ABOUT LAUREN'S LANGUAGE LESSONS

Lauren's Language Lessons is an online language school offering a variety of private and small group lessons in 10 languages including English, Korean, French, German, Italian, Portuguese, Japanese, Mandarin, Arabic, and Spanish. With Lauren's Language Lessons, you can start a new language from scratch, pick up where you left off, or perfect where you are now. All language instructors are native speakers or speak with native level fluency and accent and hold qualifications and teaching experience within their language. Private Korean lessons are offered year-round and are customized to the goals of each student to achieve the best results. We also offer small group classes with maximums of 4-6 students periodically throughout the year. Please visit our website at LaurensLanguageLessons.com or send us an email at LaurensLanguageLessons@gmail.com to learn more!

ABOUT THE TRANSLATOR

Yire emigrated from South Korea to the United States in 2003 as a high school student in Houston, Texas. She graduated from Klein High School and earned a BA in Education from the University of Texas at Austin. Since then, she has resided in Austin, Texas with her husband and two sons.

ABOUT THE AUTHOR & TRANSLATOR

Many years before the writing of this book, Lauren and Yire met in high school and quickly became close friends. Yire was Lauren's first Korean friend, and Lauren was Yire's first American friend. Lauren helped Yire get accustomed to American life, and Yire introduced Lauren to Korean food and culture and encouraged Lauren's love for all things and people international. They are honored to have this opportunity to work together to promote better understanding of their cultures and languages through this book.

www.ingramcontent.com/pod-product-compliance
Lightning Source LLC
Chambersburg PA
CBHW060916120626
46553CB00001B/353